Content With a *Whisper*

A Quest to Love God

Dr. Larry Hostetler

Unless otherwise indicated all Biblical quotations are taken
from the New Revised Standard Version Bible, copyright 1989,
Division of Christian Education of the National Council of the
Churches of Christ in the United States of America.
Used by permission. All rights reserved.

Copyright © 2010 Dr. Larry Hostetler
All rights reserved.

ISBN: 1453739718
ISBN-13: 9781453739716

I dedicate this book to my loving wife, Marion, who has been my partner in ministry and calling people to love God for over forty years, and

To Dr. Richard Phillips, "Prof," who walked with me through the valley of the shadow of unbelief, believing I would embrace God on the other side, and

To Nick Wetzel, my childhood friend whose spirit touched my spirit as a youth, and with whom I look forward to enjoying the next life.

Contents

Acknowledgements vii

Preface - Loving the Mountains ix

PART I - GROWING UP WITH GOD

Chapter I		Headed for a Collision 1

Chapter II		God Must Be Real 13

Chapter III		If I Could See the Pillar and Cloud 29

Chapter IV		God of All Ages..49

PART II – LIFE THROUGH THE EYES OF GOD

Chapter V		Loving God's Work 63

Chapter VI		Seeing Life Through the Eyes of God 77

Chapter VII		Loving Means Listening..........................93

Chapter VIII	Loving without Seeing..........................109

PART III – LOVE IN THE BIBLE

Chapter IX	God's Love for Man in Genesis	127
Chapter X	Love to a Thousand Generations	145
Chapter XI	The Pinnacle of Love – Jesus	159
Chapter XII	Love and the Commandments	173
Conclusion	The Father's Business	193

Acknowledgements

I offer my heartfelt thanks to the companions of my journey with God, the members of Chaparral Christian Church, who have wandered with me in the wilderness of anticipation from the early days of the Church. Marion and I have enjoyed a spiritual (and often lavish) banquet with God's finest people for over three decades.

I thank my dear fellow searchers in High Flight, a class that dares to go to the edge of God's Canyon of Love and peer into its depths while sometimes enjoying the resulting vertigo.

I especially want to thank my children, Bly and Karla, Sharon, and Jackie and Tom for being the most wondrous expressions of God's love a father could ever have.

I offer my deep gratitude to my dear friends, Charles and Danielle Rouiller, on whose balcony at their Bed and Breakfast near Gruyere, Switzerland, much of this book was written. Their hospitality was gracious and generous, their patience with my stumbling French an international gift, and Danielle's food a lasting treasure of Swiss cuisine. They are dear brother and sister.

Finally, and most profoundly, I am grateful to the family of my childhood, starting with my father, Harry Blythe Hostetler, the man who taught me to love God while digging potatoes, hunting mushrooms, hiking into Havasupi Canyon, watching soaring birds, telling and reading stories, and a hundred other things that only a father can do for his children. My heartfelt thanks to my mother, Opal Iola Hostetler for her surpassing love, courage and determination, and for being the best mother a son could wish for, to my sisters and brother: Nancy White who is smiling down from heaven, Dr. Jerry Hostetler who is my big little brother, Kay Cook who makes me very proud, and to Edith McNeilly who on behalf of God loves those entrusted to her care.

Preface - Loving the Mountains

A Canyon of Thought. I began writing the following little muse on April 18, 2007, and have returned to it many times in order to contemplate the canyon of thought which it represents in me. As I bring to an end this verbal painting on "Loving God" I am reminded that all these words mock my attempt to capture even a rough sketch of the reality of loving God. I feel kindred thoughts with the Psalmist who wrote, "When I consider the works of Your hands, what is man that You are mindful of him?" (Psalm 8:4)

Thoughts from Charles and Danielle Rouiller's Balcony
Switzerland - October 9, 2009

Sitting on a balcony I look out over an awesome Alps-scape that I cannot possibly paint with words grand and beautiful enough to capture them. I can't even take an adequate mental photograph that projects on the screen of my brain for even an instant after I close my eyes. A few weeks from now those inadequate mental snapshots will have taken on a dream-like quality that will bring pleasure accompanied by a longing to return to their reality. The poet describes it well in these words:

> For oft, when on my couch I lie
> In vacant or in pensive mood,
> They flash upon that inward eye

> Which is the bliss of solitude;
> And then my heart with pleasure fills,
> And dances with the daffodils.
> -William Wordsworth,
>   "I Wandered Lonely As a Cloud"

Wordsworth's "inward eye" does, indeed, give me pleasure in my memory, but I have to be there in the presence of the mountains to dance.

Some things are just too wonderful to capture in words, whether images or the precious moments of life or the feelings of love. So I must accept the reality that my attempts to capture the meaning of loving God in words is probably a quixotic quest which, while irresistible, will fall far short of realization. No problem. In some ways the quest is enough in itself. I imagine that if I could capture in words what it means to love God I would be disappointed. It would not live up to my expectations of experiencing God fully. Along with the Apostle Paul I must say that I see God only dimly. I yearn to see Him clearly and without hindrance. That does not come for humans until journey's end.

It's like the mountain scenes which continue to pull my eye away from the screen of my computer as I type these words. What I see as I gaze on those ethereal scenes beyond me stuns my inner being into an almost hypnotic trance. On the one hand those scenes saturate my capacity to perceive. In the same moment I realize it is far more than I can process given the senses available to me. I have climbed up into those mountains, tasted their frigid, plunging water and smelled their brilliant flowers. I've been startled by resident wild creatures into whose living room I've intruded. I've looked with envy at raptors, lifted by invisible currents of air, soaring high above where they scan for the day's meal in the meadows and forests where I walk.

I ask myself if I have really seen or come close to totally experiencing this vast landscape which is portrayed before me in pigments of wood, stone, snow, grass, clouds and a hundred other mediums used by its Artist to fill in the canvas spread before me. I am aware even while soaking it all in that I see only a speck, if it can be called even that, of the totality being registered on my brain, on my whole being. Yet I offer myself as one more medium on which to record the vast range of strokes made by The Artist's brush.

I love these mountains, valleys and streams. I love being here among them. I love being overwhelmed by their unfathomable niches, each a galaxy unto itself. I say I love this infinitely diverse microcosm of the universe even while realizing I experience it as a mostly blind person with an amoeba's brain. To say I love the mountains is a wistful exaggeration for I know that I don't even begin to comprehend and experience them...well, maybe begin, but barely.

To love a niche of the earth is to recognize that I'm not required to know it's every molecule or even its every element and organism in order to appreciate it. Neither is it to pretend that its steep cliffs are accessible to me or that being lost in its depths could not injure or even kill me. I love it from the safe balcony or the easy trail during the warmth of day. I would fear its hidden dangers if lost in the dark or perched on an inaccessible eyrie.

What is this love I feel for the mountains? It's a response of awe at what is before me. At the same time it's an acknowledgement of that which is lacking within me. My consciousness is expanded by the magnitude of that which is so much greater and wondrous than I. Yet the mountains cannot love in return, for they lack what my species singularly brings to it. Even the birds that soar above and the animals which thrive in the bosom of its forests experience their reality only fractionally compared to humans, or so I imagine.

What does it mean to love mountains? For a bird? For an elk? For a human? For God? Only God can probe to every tiny crevasse, to every mountain pool where lurks the granddaddy of all trout, to the mother lode of gold and diamonds—to the heart of the mountain. I cannot love the mountains as they deserve to be loved. How can I love the One Who does love them as they deserve? I'm doing my best. It will have to be enough.

There was a time when I loved God with my whole being. Then my being was much less than it is now. It was still me—totally me, but my ten-year-old being was very limited in scope of knowledge, experience and awareness. When I was a child, I thought as a child. Now that I am a man I do not wish to put away childish things, but to expand my awareness to adult dimensions as fully as I imagine I did to my child dimensions. How do I love God now?

PART I
Growing Up With God

I.
Headed for a Collision

God in the Potato Patch. There we were, dad and I, digging potatoes out in the family garden in Central Illinois. It wasn't my favorite job under any circumstances, but I especially didn't like it on Saturday morning. I was tortured by the thought of my friends riding their bicycles through the maple tunnels of colored autumn leaves. They would be playing marbles or mumbly peg, maybe even fishing in Rhodes Creek.

I was digging my hands into the dirt trying to find all the potatoes that seemed to be doing their best to hide in the black Illinois soil. My dad had a four-tined garden fork that he pushed into the ground a respectful distance from the now-dead potato vine. He was a muscular man who supported his family of five children by working in an iron foundry all week. Effortlessly he turned over the soil and out would roll juicy spuds—buried treasure from the ground. My job was to pick out every big and little spud, rub the dirt off, and put it in the bushel basket I pulled as I crawled behind him.

I loved potatoes. I knew if we got enough they would last through the winter, snuggly sheltered in our cellar. My mother worked magic with them. Potatoes and gravy are still among my favorite foods. Every once in a while my dad would spear one, which always aggravated him because he knew it wouldn't last the winter. I didn't mind because I knew it meant plenty of potatoes in the next couple of weeks. We had to eat the wounded potatoes before they spoiled.

I always started these harvests in a grumpy mood. Saturdays were play days for most kids. Not for Blythe Hostetler's oldest son. Oh, no! He was pressed into forced labor. It just wasn't fair.

After an hour or so of digging and putting up with my grumbling, my patient and understanding father had cajoled me into feeling maybe I was the privileged "older brother." He confided in me that his life had not been so easy either. Growing up in Colorado had been hard. Later I learned he had spent only a couple of years in Colorado, but somehow there in the potato patch those years expanded into his entire childhood. Funny, isn't it, how an especially impressionable experience can define an entire stage of life?

Life really had been tough for him, even in the idyllic setting of the mountains. He entertained me with stories of catching trout in a nearby lake, climbing trees to see eagles' nests up close, and hiking and playing in the enchanting mountain forest. Oh, I forgot myself.... Life was tough. His dad, my grandfather, was the minister of a small mountain church. How they got by with a dozen children on a meager salary I couldn't imagine.

Once, a coal train derailed a couple of miles away from their cabin. In spite of a badly sprained ankle he took the family wheelbarrow and gathered some of the spilt coal. No, he wasn't stealing, he assured me. The railroad permitted this "help" with the cleanup. What a luxury to his eleven siblings to have a few days of warmth. I began to think I didn't have it so rough after all. He learned to love God in the shadow of the mystical Pike's Peak.

It was there in the potato patch on the fertile plains of Illinois, hands blackened from brushing the dirt off the potatoes, I think I saw my dad's soul. What I discovered while sifting through the dirt was a man I loved dearly, digging potatoes out of the ground because he wanted to feed his five hungry children. He talked about learning to love God with eleven brothers and sisters while trying to survive in the awesome yet foreboding mountain wilderness. Survival meant filling the cellar with the small potatoes that would grow in that rocky soil. It fed them through the snow-covered winter.

By comparison, dirty hands and five or six nice potatoes from each hill in rich Illinois soil didn't seem so bad. God gave these potatoes to people who loved Him. How could I complain about picking up such riches? Eyes still searching for every hiding potato I said, "Dad, when I grow up, I hope I love God as much as you do."

In response to my six-year-old wish to love God as much as my dad did, he assured me I would love God at least as much as he did. I determined to try. I may someday love God as much as he did. I will never love Him the same as did my father, for I think we all love God differently. If it were the same for everyone I don't think it would be love.

I Loved God Then. I think I was born with an awareness of God. It just came naturally. I had a passionate desire to understand Him, to please Him from a very early age. I felt odd—that I was different from the other children. Why didn't they care about God the way I did? My sisters and brother were brought up in the same family and none of them had a God passion, at least not like mine. Why not? Why did I? I don't know. I just did. I now believe God put a love for Himself in my heart. It's the only way I can explain it.

My brother and three sisters attended Church as often as I did, and I'm happy to say they were and are good and successful people. I think it not unfair, nor do I mean it to be diminishing, to say of them that their interest in God didn't run as deep as mine. My interest in God caused me to want to become a minister. Their interests led them to other worthy vocations. God comes to each of us in unique ways and at different times. This diversity in the way we understand God is fascinating and a part of the wonder of being human.

For me, there in the potato patch, I began a life-long search that has not ended yet. It's not merely a search FOR God. It's more a search to know God, and to understand His love. My happy quest is to fully experience and be aware of, not only God's love for me, but of my love for God and what that means. An important part of that quest is to invite others to join in the journey.

How is it possible for a human being to love God? We say we love God, in fact are commanded to love God. But what does that mean? How can a human being, so pathetically limited compared to God, claim to express anything remotely approaching love for God, the creator of the universe? One thing I knew in my childhood. I wanted to love God as much as my dad loved Him.

For my dad, loving God meant going to church every Sunday, giving a tithe—yes, one-tenth—of the hard-earned money he made working in an iron foundry, and praying every night. On most nights he read Bible stories to his children before we went to bed. Some nights after he thought we were all asleep, I would see him kneeling in prayer in front of the one over-stuffed chair we had. He taught a Sunday school class, discussed religion with friends and neighbors, and talked about God with his son while digging potatoes.

I loved God when I was a child. I really loved Him. I knew what it meant to love Him then. I wish I had written it down while I still knew the secret. It never occurred to me that I'd ever feel less clear about what loving Him meant. I just loved Him. That love shaped who I was and determined how I lived my life. I prayed often, read the Bible almost daily, and attended church every Sunday. Perhaps most uniquely for a youth, I thought about God a lot. I think it not an exaggeration to say that my mind was fixed on God. He shaped my life and guided my decisions.

When riding my bike I imagined God surrounding me. When I went fishing in the creek I felt God there with me, perhaps guiding a fish toward my bait. When I came home with a string full of less than God-sized fish, my mother would cook them for dinner. I loved God for providing food. In school I knew God filled my mind with the things I needed to remember. While playing basketball I sensed God smiling at my agility and being pleased when I made a basket.

Engineer and Preacher. At some point I began to think about what I would do when I grew up. The most spectacular event each day was the nearly hourly plunge of the New York Central freight trains through the middle of our tiny town. They didn't even slow down. They were that important. Their approach could be heard as they whistled in the distance. When they reached the outskirts of town the twin lights on the warning signal would start to flash, back and forth, on-off, on-off, a bell on the signal would begin to clang its warning and the guard gate would lower.

The engineer, leaning out of the smoke-belching locomotive, often smiled and waved at the awe-stricken children as he thundered by. I never tired of the spectacle. To control such an awesome piece of machinery seemed to me the pinnacle of the exciting life—God and me sweeping through the Illinois countryside. That, and—by the time I was in fourth grade—I knew I wanted to be a preacher. I would thunder over the tracks during the week and thunder from the pulpit on Sundays.

The thirty to forty-minute sermons every Sunday were for me the most important time of the week. To passionately call people to devotion to God and away from the destructive ways of the devil was the highest and greatest thing a person could do. To save people from hell became for me a passion. To save myself from hell became almost an obsession. My behavior was guided by trying to avoid thoughts or actions that would send me to hell. Surely if I helped other people escape hell, I would avoid its burning fires myself.

There developed this tension between love and fear. I knew that God loved me—I sang songs that told me so, read His Word that assured me that He saw me as His child, and told my friends how important it was for them to serve God. I dreamed of preaching to a church full of people, exhorting them to follow God and escape eternal punishment in hell.

My love for God caused me to enjoy the beauty and wonder of life. I loved life and that was a part of my love for God. It still is. My fear of God caused me to worry about my eternal destination and the fate of my friends and family. I still fear God but it is a fear of awe and not terror.

I was barely aware of the paradox within. God loves me. YET, if I'm not good, He sends me to hell. Love God so you won't go to hell. It made sense to me then. It never occurred to me that love and fear (as in terror) just don't go together. I have come to see that God wants love—real honest to goodness love, that is based on His incomparable love for us. "There is no fear in love. But perfect love drives out fear..." (1 Jn. 4:18). I'm still pursuing that perfect love.

Train Wreck. I went to a Christian College to prepare to be a minister. How much more can a person love God than that? Here I was studying the Bible every day, giving up my dream of being a railway engineer, planning to devote my life to saving people from the fires of hell. I knew exactly what a person had to do to earn God's love. The formula was simple—Follow and understand God just the way I had been taught.

That was the problem. I loved God as I had defined Him, and boy did I have Him figured out. As I studied I realized there were some things about this God that bothered me. How could He accept only those who were fortunate enough to have been born into my Church, the one true way? I believed that people who went to other churches and followed God differently from what I had been taught were lost. I'm not sure if that is what I was taught or if I came to that view on my own. I was sure that only a few select people were going to make it into heaven. I saw myself as one of the oh-so-lucky elect.

The first few years of college confirmed my certainty in the one true way. Then one night in the seminary library I was reading a book that stopped me in my tracks. The author stated that the more certain a person is that their view of something is the only correct view, the more likely the person is to be insecure in that view. It hit me like a freight train—I the victim, not the engineer! I was passionate in holding that I was right about God and other people were wrong. Was it possible that my brash certainty was a mask for deep uncertainty? I knew in a moment that my insecurity had arisen to do battle with me.

My narrow and bigoted view of God had a strong grip on me. In classes taught by a new professor, Richard Phillips, I became aware that he had gone through a similar painful awakening to the one I was experiencing. I talked to him about my growing doubts and difficulties with God as I understood Him. It was okay to question my view of God, he assured me. God didn't mind being scrutinized. Considering alternative views of God was not only acceptable, it was the only way to really know God. That was scary—and liberating.

I had heard preachers and professors vilify "liberal" Christians as Godless enemies of the one true way. These liberals dared to examine and question fundamental truths that had already been fully and finally determined. They asked questions that were troubling. I had seen them as the enemy to be defeated in their satanic views.

Was it possible I could learn something from our differences? Where better to consider alternative views of God than in one of their seminaries? I asked Dr. Phillips which was the best seminary, the most highly regarded. He pointed me to New York City and Union Theological Seminary, the "liberal stronghold of America." I decided to storm the fortress of the enemy. I would show them the true way or perish trying.

Into the Lion's Den. For three years I confronted the doubts that had assaulted my mind, and explored many new questions about God. I dissected the God of my childhood, then attempted to reconstruct my view of God in this very open-minded community of faith in the middle of a huge metropolis.

I studied the Old Testament with Samuel Terrien, who didn't even believe that Moses had written the entire first five books of the Bible! How far from God can a man get—to deny that Moses wrote every word of the Pentateuch? Incongruously, the prayers with which this liberal foe began every class reflected a deep love and regard for the God of those pages. Professor Terrien loved the writings of the Old Testament, not for who wrote them but for the precious truth they revealed. I heard the Spirit of God in his prayers...could not deny Its Presence.

Other professors, including Reinhold Niebuhr, Roger Shinn, and Eberhard Bethge, opened my eyes to the ethical dilemmas of life that have no easy answers. W. D. Davies forced me to think of the human link in bringing us the Gospels. It was so hard to give up the notion that God had simply dictated the words to Matthew and the rest.

There were times when I didn't like God—no longer cared for Him at all. How could this One whom I had loved so much deceive me so thoroughly? If there was a God why did He make life so difficult? Why was there so much evil and suffering in the world? It's never easy to give up cherished childhood truths. I didn't let go of mine without a fearful and painful struggle.

The liberal professors weren't the only ones who scandalized my view of God. There was a fellow student from Holland, a Jesuit priest, who talked about loving God. Imagine that! A CATHOLIC, and a priest at that, who talked about loving the God Who had revealed himself exclusively and uniquely to my Church and me.

I went to interfaith meetings across the street at Jewish Theological Seminary. Rabbis and their students talked about the

God Who I knew had little regard for them. After all, they had rejected His Son. Yet, unaccountably, they were passionate in their search for God and claimed He had called them to serve Him. I didn't find it pleasant to learn of new dimensions of God from Catholics and Jews. How could they claim to know the God Who had chosen only people like me?

It's not really painful for me to look back and see how incredibly bigoted and naïve I was. In some ways my narrowness focused my spirit and energy—perhaps provided the velocity that hurled me into the wondrous vastness and variety of God's love. Yes, it was distressing at the time—dreadful even—to confront my pride and arrogance revealed in juxtaposition to those whom I had once scorned and vilified. My roots remained firm in the fertile soil of my childhood, but I felt the branches of a maturing faith begin to spread.

Collision with God. Out of this traumatic train wreck, with the God of the larger world outside my little Illinois garden-spot, emerged a new understanding of the incredible breadth and diverse dimensions of God. It was the God of my childhood Who saturated my spirit. It was the God of the whole world Who won my devotion.

I did not let go of my exclusive franchise on God easily. It was a long and sometimes frightening journey as I dealt with the inner conflicts. It was as though a dark cloud descended over my whole being. I couldn't concentrate. I couldn't sleep. At times I almost couldn't stand the deep agony of my soul. In the middle of the night I would often try to escape my pain by going out in the foreboding streets of New York City. Somehow in walking through the dark forest of buildings I would find a certain release and could survive another day.

For those who have not gone through this type of "dark night of the soul" (see: "The Confessions of Saint Augustine," Book VIII, Paragraphs 28 and 29), I can tell you, it's the most agonizing, consuming, and debilitating condition I have ever experienced. The physical and mental anguish are beyond describing and unimaginable unless you've gone through it. It is also, I've come to learn, the most creative, mind-expanding, altering of a failed reality that I believe is humanly possible. The darkness descends and after what seems an eternity, a glimmer of light begins to emerge.

There was no moment of break-through, no burning bush, no voice out of heaven, or vision in the night. There was a gradual dawning of a new day in my life. The darkness slowly lifted and the pain diminished. I didn't realize it for some years, but somehow the God of the potato patch and the God of the city streets shook hands and embraced my heart, my being. I wouldn't have missed it for anything.

It is the God with Whom I have argued and struggled and walked for almost seven decades Whom I wish to love with all my heart, soul, mind and strength. In these pages I hope to express what it means to me to love Him. I hope, even more, to help others discover their own unique love and relationship with their heavenly Father…to perhaps collide with God and then…if they are up to it, to be captured by God.

II.
God Must Be Real

In an Airplane Galley Over Greenland. Baruch, of Safid, Israel, distinct in his Orthodox Jewish garb, shares a long night of trans-Atlantic flight in the galley of the airplane with two brothers and me. The two brothers are on their way to Poland to attend their grandmother's funeral. I am on my way to Switzerland to study and write. Standing together in the cramped space of the galley stretching our legs we exchange friendly chitchat at, God knows, what time of night. In Chicago, where we embarked over four hours ago, it's now 9 p.m. In Frankfurt, our next stop, it's 4 a.m. What time it is over the Atlantic has no meaning. We are time travelers suspended somewhere in no-time. We are restless, unable to sleep in the crowded plane, each with our own thoughts of the time to which we go.

Baruch tells us he has been to the wedding of a friend in Chicago. For him it's a rushed trip consisting of as many hours of travel as of celebration. He arrived in Chicago day before yesterday. Yesterday was the wedding. Today he returns to Israel by way of Frankfurt. He has another long flight after Frankfurt ahead of him. He asks, perhaps out of politeness, what takes me to Frankfurt. I reply that I'm actually going to Switzerland by way of Frankfurt and that my purpose in going is to spend some time working on a book. "What book?" he asks. "A book on 'What Does It Mean To Love God?'" I tell him. He nods, somewhat dismissively.

"Are you Orthodox?" I ask to be sure. "Yes," he acknowledges. "I am Christian," I tell him. "We are brothers." "That is a broad statement," he replies warily. "I do not mean it to be broad. You and I are believers in, and children of, the same God. We both acknowledge Him as Father. Am I right? I believe we are brothers." He merely nods, the sideways nod of neutral noncommittal. I persist. "I am Christian, but I accept you as brother in the family of God, and hope that you acknowledge me in the same way." Again, the noncommittal nod.

A flight attendant tells us she needs to work in our part of the galley, and will we go to the other side, please. Baruch and I go. The brothers return to their seats. "So, what does it mean to you to love God, Baruch?" "It is not an easy thing to say," he ponders aloud. I wait, listening. "I have not put it into words," he confesses. "It's a concept I accept, but have not described."

I told him of the many people I've talked to about loving God. Most have difficulty answering, and are hesitant to try to put it into words, I tell him. He nods again, this time a nod of understanding. "Do you love God?" I ask.

"Yes," he replies. "But for me that has several levels." He looks within himself then continues. "The first level is that God must be real. It is not so much a matter of believing IN God, but of experiencing God. One must experience God within."

"Do you have children?" he asks.
"Three, and ten grandchildren," I shamelessly brag.

"I have thirteen children," he proudly reveals. "The last two were twins. My wife was an only child. Go figure. My name means 'blessing' in Hebrew." I sense he is glad to be a blessing. I sense also that he is, perhaps subconsciously, relating one of the ways he experiences God—through his children.

"Man makes himself God," he ventures. "The Torah tells of Satan saying, 'You will be like God.' So the problem today is that everyone thinks they are God. That is what is wrong with the world."

I thank him for indulging me in my questions, and for his answer. "God must be real." There, in an airplane defying gravity at 37,000 feet above Iceland, God, Who according to some defies reason, was real. Today, a day later, Baruch is among his thirteen children, and perhaps they are aware that God is real to their father. And they will love their father and our Father. They will experience God in their father.

Experiencing God. "God must be real." For Baruch that did not mean merely believing IN God, but experiencing God within. At that point in the flight everyone was asked to return to their seats. I didn't have the opportunity to ask him what makes God real to him. His children—all thirteen—are a part of his experience of God. The Torah is also a part of his experience of God, since a reference to Torah was his next thought after his children. How we experience God is a key concept in understanding how we love God and what that love means.

"What does it mean to you to love God?" I've asked many people that question. The reactions vary from those who are indignant that I would even ask such a question, to those who acknowledge they've never really thought about it. Many have confessed that they want to love God, know they are supposed to, but that it's not an easy question after all. A Swiss mother said loving God meant going to mass every Sunday. I suspected she was saying that for the benefit of her daughter and son-in-law, who were also at the dinner table, and who did not go to mass at all.

Others have said they love God because of all He does for them. They have experienced God in the adventure and joy of life. Loving God and loving life were for them synonymous. It isn't that they felt God had favored them any more than others. For them God has favored all humans with this wonderful awareness called life.

I've also known people who expressed anger at God. How could they love a God Who allowed terrible things to happen to innocent people, especially children? For them the experience of a terrible event in which God had failed to intervene convinced them that either God did not exist, or if He did exist they could not love One Who stood by and allowed such tragedy. How could they love, or even believe in a God like that?

I have been persistent in asking my question, and frequently rewarded with insightful and helpful replies. The varieties of ways in which people experience God have similarities, but also great diversity. Prayer, meditation, reading the Bible, music, art, great events, joyful experiences and important people in their lives have all been mentioned as ways in which people experience God.

The influential people in a person's life have frequently been the central factor in a person's experience of God. I read somewhere that Martin Luther said, "I see God most clearly in the lives of other people." This has been true in my own experience. My father, ministers in our Church, friends, professors, my grandmother, and many others have added to my experience of God. God first became real as I saw Him through their eyes.

One of the reasons I decided to attend a multi-denominational Seminary was that I wanted to associate with men and women who were asking the same questions about God that I was asking. I wanted to hear how they had dealt with those questions and remained devoted to God. I wanted to see if they saw something of God that had eluded me. I believe that all people who earnestly seek to know God see a part of Him that would benefit my own experience of God.

Listening with All Available Ears. From the time I was a little boy I've listened for direction from God with all available ears. Yes, like the boy Samuel, I listened for His voice in the night. I mean that literally. If I listened, surely God would reward my attention with an unmistakable word. Though it never came there was still the experience of listening, which was satisfying in its own way—I don't know why. The silence did not disappoint me so much as it caused me to long more deeply for some whisper from God. I listened as a little boy, and have never stopped listening. I listen still.

The experience of God is very real to those who love Him. He is experienced in "a sound of sheer silence" (1 Ki. 19:12), or as the KJV has it, the "still small voice." "A still small voice," accurate translation or not, more accurately describes my own experience. Standing at the base of Havasu Falls in Arizona the sound is deafening, yet there is a still small voice. A coyote howls in the distant hills, accompanied by a still small voice. In the first words of my children - "Da-Da" there is a still small voice. In the flash of lightning, the roll of thunder, the first chirping of the birds in the morning, a performance of Handel's Messiah, and a hundred other sounds. If you don't believe that, then I don't know what other contact you have with the Almighty, but I believe you're missing out on one of the most important parts of the relationship He wants to have with you—momentary "a-ha experiences," or epiphanies.

Did God speak only to men of old? Why would He stop? Have we outgrown our need to hear His voice? Or have our ears turned to stone so we can no longer hear? Do we hear, but not understand? Is the surrounding noise of life so loud that when God speaks, as in a crowded, noisy room, the best we're able to muster is an impatient, "Huh?"

A woman I met only once told me there are times in her life when God seems to "get involved." "When that happens," she related, "I know I'm probably going to go through a time that shapes me and changes me. After a while it's as though God says to me, 'Okay, you're on the right track now. You're on your own.' I'm always open to God getting involved but He seems to do it only when I need some direction."

I'm not sure if God speaks or "gets involved" so unmistakably that we would distinguish His words, or even recognize that it was Him guiding or showing up. I can say with some certainty that God has led, and is leading, my journey. I experience the reality of God in His direction in my life. It began in a tiny village in central Illinois. It was, as my niece describes it, "a place where you go to watch the grass grow." Yet it was also a place where God took hold of me. He got involved with me. I even knew it as it happened.

By the fourth grade I knew I wanted to be a preacher. Don't ask me how I knew, but I knew. There was no voice of God saying, "Go preach Christ," no burning bush, no light blazing out of heaven...just a quiet understanding between God and me that trickled into my heart.

I knew I saw the world differently from most of my friends. I wanted to be good. I wanted to please God. It mattered to me. I wanted to help others see God. All right, I must admit that some of it was guilt over real and, more often, imagined sins. There was some fear—okay, a lot of fear. I must confess to having a vivid sense of the fires of hell, and the expectation of the return of Christ "on the clouds of the sky."

But it wasn't fear that drove me, at least that's not what I recall. It was simply that I knew I wanted to follow God, to be His messenger and His servant. I didn't work at it. I didn't worry it. I didn't look around for signs. I simply felt it. God was real to me. He still is.

It Runs In My Family. One of my associates was asked by a parent to meet with her seven-year-old son to talk about being baptized. In our congregation it is an important part of our theology that a person being baptized understands the meaning and symbolism of what they are doing. The usual age where we feel this is possible is somewhere between ten and thirteen. With a lad of only seven years some extra scrutiny was called for.

"So, why do you want to be baptized?" asked my associate. "Because I love God," came the confident reply. "And why do you love God?"

The child thought a moment and said, "I guess it just sort of runs in our family."

Maybe an awareness of God is in my genes. My grandfather Hostetler was a preacher, and my grandmother a Christian "teacher." I didn't know my grandfather, who died when I was too young to remember. My grandmother Hostetler was an important presence in my life. She helped shaped my life. She came to stay in our home for a few weeks when I was very little. I remember how she spoke with conviction of her experiences with God. It was very natural to her.

Later, she lived in a little house that was on my way home from grade school. I would often stop to see her, and she would reward me with cookies and milk. Sometimes she would give me little American Bible Institute Scripture portions. When she saw I appreciated them she began to give me a few at a time. Soon I had the whole Bible—that's right...the WHOLE Bible in little individual booklets.

I remember her telling me that her "life verse" was, "And this is life eternal, that they might know Thee the only true God, and Jesus Christ, whom thou hast sent"—yes, in the King James Version (Jn. 17:3). She said God had given that to her as her special "life verse," and that perhaps God would give one to me as well. I wanted a life verse of my very own, but didn't rush it. I was content to wait for the gift should it come.

Somewhere in college a verse emerged and I knew it was one of the defining concepts of my life—"Eye has not seen, nor ear heard, neither has it entered the heart of man the things that God has prepared for those who love Him" (I Cor. 2:9, RSV). My love for God, and the reality of God for me, has been shaped by that concept.

I have looked for God with my eyes. I've listened for Him with my ears. I've seen and heard Him, less with my eyes or ears, but more with my heart. He's that real.

Wise men and women guided me. I could list so many...my father and mother, a professor, friends and also opponents. They were, and are in part, truly the voice of God to me. God was real to some of them. I experienced God's guidance in what I experienced in all of them. They have helped to make God come alive—to become real, for me.

God In Scripture. Scripture shaped my awareness of God. My dad read Bible stories to his children. I read the portions of Scripture my grandmother gave me, and studied the Bible in Sunday school. I listened for what it would say to my spirit. I was deeply impressed by the story of Solomon asking for wisdom instead of riches. I thought, "If it could work for Solomon...." Well, I asked for wisdom. I remember doing it—asking straight out, "Dear Father, give me the gift of wisdom."

From then on I stayed alert to see if the gift was being given. In the meantime I tried to be wise. Whether I was given wisdom or not I cannot say. I know I've tried to be wise in my dealings and decisions, and just trying to be wise has often been enough. Desiring a gift from God frequently results in receiving the gift. Reading of Solomon's experience helped shaped my experience of the reality of God.

The Bible records the history of God's interaction with His people from Adam through Jesus and through the early days of the Church. The history of God's dealing with His people continues. It didn't stop after the last word of Scripture was written. But Scripture remains as the core of thousands of years of people's experiences with God. The Bible has continued to enjoy the affirmation people of faith who wish to walk with God.

The past experiences of the people of God are a valuable gauge of our own experiences. Those who listen for God must be certain that when a word comes to them that it's verified by more than their own judgment. The saints of old are a measuring "cloud of witnesses" in this process. Scripture is a record of God's leading in the past and a guide to how He still leads us.

Scripture is also a sharp chisel which shapes who we are and who we are becoming. Those who would listen to God had better be prepared to go through some painful reshaping of who they are. The voice of God is more often a prod than a praise. While listening for God one must be expecting the hammer of the Sculptor.

The stories of the Bible helped make God real to me. I've already related my experience in connection with Solomon's request for wisdom. David taught me God's courage in the face of evil giants. He also convinced me of the reality of God's forgiveness of even murder and adultery. Joseph encouraged me to be a Godly dreamer. Even the murderous Cain revealed the God of, "If at first you don't succeed, try, try again."

It was Jesus Who made the God of the resurrection a reality for me. God must be very real to one if they are willing to die for Him. Laying down one's life for a friend who is seen is equated with laying down one's life for God Who is not seen. In baptism the reality of the new life and the reality of the Spirit of God are experienced. Our own story of life with God becomes as real as that of the saints.

The commands and instructions that are recorded in the Bible provide guidance in what other people of God believed to be the Godly way of life. These commands and instructions were examined in the unfolding experience of each new development in their history. Some of the specifics changed over the years, though the Spirit remained the same. (We don't typically greet one another with a holy kiss or wash each other's feet. Our culture has different graces.) That concept bounces off the pedestal upon which Christians sometimes place the Bible, but it's nevertheless true. The Bible is a growing record of people's real-life experiences with God.

Danger In Words Written in Stone. There is a danger in understanding Scripture as the leading of God. That danger is the temptation to see it as the only word, a kind of final determining of reality between God and man that resists searching any deeper or wider. If God has already spoken His perfect, infallible and final Word, then why look any farther? Indeed, looking farther might be seen as failing to give due honor to that word already given.

Further compounding this danger is the reality that it isn't as simple as accepting what the Scripture says. Scripture always comes to us through the filter of our own fallible understanding and interpretation. Only the Pope claims infallibility in interpretation, leading me to two inescapable realities: (1) I am not the Pope, and (2) The Pope is not God.

Some of the changes in the way people experienced God are very evident in the Biblical record. Through much of the Old Testament times animal sacrifices were commanded and practiced. Most Jewish people no longer observe those commands, and I know of no Christians who do. The Christian view of God is that the sacrifice of God's Son made animal sacrifices no longer necessary. There is a continuing thread of the Spirit found in Paul's admonition, "to present your bodies as a living sacrifice, holy and acceptable to God..." (Rom. 12:1).

There are other changes. Christians no longer celebrate the Sabbath, the observance of which is one of the Ten Commandments. The first day of the week, the Lord's Day, has replaced the Sabbath. In the early days of the Church Christians met daily and in each other's houses to celebrate the resurrection. That has changed to a once weekly celebration. The celebration of Christmas, Ash Wednesday, Good Friday and Lent are some examples of the adaptive practices in which people worship God. The experience of loving God is a living, dynamic and growing relationship.

Some things have not changed. Most Jewish people continue to celebrate the ancient feasts—the Passover, the Day of Atonement, the Festival of Booths, and others. Many other ancient holidays are an important part of present day Judaism. Some of these are also celebrated by Christians, such as the Feast of the Passover, which we have transformed into the Lord's Supper. The reality of God is experienced and celebrated differently in these celebrations by the communities of Godly people.

How limiting it would be if we were not encouraged to push new frontiers and deepen our understanding of what it means to be children of God. God did not create us to simply have the same experiences over and over. Each experience opens exponentially expanding experiences that grow out of each new experience. God's leading is consistent with the past, yet unpredictable in its creative expanding possibilities.

Scripture is not a closed record of God's experience with His people. It is a complete Word from God as far as it goes. It is not, however, the final reality between God and man. Scripture instructs us to search deeper and wider, although always within the parameters it establishes. Paul instructs, "Work out your own salvation with fear and trembling; for it is God Who is at work in you, enabling you both to will and to work for His good pleasure" (Phil. 2:12, 13).

God is as real now as He was to those who delivered His Word in Scripture. If the final word from God has been given, it would mean that God is less real to us than He was to those whose experiences are recorded in Scripture. It would dishonor and diminish what God has accomplished in the past if His people today did not experience His reality in new journeys to yet unrealized promised lands. In a sense, we are all in Ur of the Chaldeans (Gen. 11:31 - 12:4). In a sense we all have heard His call to a land that He will show us. What is needed is our responding to that call with our feet, that is, by going!

God In the Community of the Church. My wife, Marion, and I founded Chaparral Christian Church in 1978, in Scottsdale, Arizona. When the Church outgrew its worship space I knew we needed to build more facilities. The Worship Center was crowded at both of our two services. We simply needed to have a larger place to worship. A board meeting was called to make the decision to build and I presented the case.

During the discussion one of our elders, who often had taken a contrarian point of view, said, "We've always said Chaparral puts children first. This doesn't do that. Our children need classrooms." My first thought was, "Classrooms will be made possible later by the increased number of people we can have in worship." I held my tongue. There was something in what the man said that deserved attention.

A very lively time of "listening to the Spirit" followed. Both sides of the issue were fully discussed. There was no doubt that more facilities were needed, but which—worship or classrooms? It was put to a vote. The decision was very nearly unanimous. Build the classrooms. We added a third worship service almost immediately, and after the classrooms were built we started a new worship center.

No One Person Has the Whole Spirit. It was such experiences as that which shaped my thinking that no one person has the whole Spirit. Jesus said, "For where two or three are gathered in my name, I am there among them" (Matt. 18:20). That concept of multiple expressions of the Spirit has provided valuable guidance through the years. Even the whole church cannot contain the whole Spirit of God, but it is more likely to embody more of the Spirit than any individual.

Any appeal to the Spirit must also be in harmony with what is taught in Scripture as studied and applied by the Church. No Scripture is of private interpretation (2 Pet. 1:20). That doesn't mean the whole Church will always get it right. It means the understanding of the whole Church is a guide that has stood the test of time. Those who would be led by God dare not ignore the work of the Spirit through the centuries. That is what the Bible represents.

Not surprisingly, through the years there have been individuals who have been critical of various decisions. They have always been listened to and their concerns addressed. During one very evident time of dissention we formulated a response to differences of opinion in general. In a sermon dealing with disagreement I noted that the Church had a four-step response to any disagreement:

1. If anyone disagrees with a decision, listen to them. They may be right.
2. A minister will meet with the person and attempt to reach an agreement.
3. If an agreement cannot be reached, the matter is to be taken to the elders.
4. The decision of the elders will be supported by the whole Church.

Following that approach was helpful, creative, and produced harmony in that instance and in every one since. Step 3 was invoked only twice, as I recall. In both instances the elders affirmed the original decision. In both instances the ones disagreeing left the Church. They were good people who saw things differently from the Church leadership. While the loss of those people was painful, I believe this approach was God's leading just as much as Jethro's advice to Moses long ago (Ex. 18:13-27). Just as importantly it acknowledged that those who love God also love and respect one another's views.

The purpose statement of Chaparral Christian Church has from the beginning been, "We exist to be the presence of Christ." We understand this to extend to our city, our country and our world. It begins with our being the presence of Christ to each other. God has become real to us in our attempt to be the presence of His Son in the world.

This reality begins with our individual experiences, and is harmonized in our listening to each other and in being guided by

Scripture. This reality is held together, not by rigid interpretation of Scripture, but by love. God has become real to us in the journey that is connected to past journeys and even wanderings, which lead always to the high calling of God in Jesus Christ (Phil. 3:12-14). The Promised Land is wherever and whenever God is experienced as real.

III.
If I Could See the Pillar and Cloud

Expecting God to Lead. One of the joys of loving God is that I expect Him to lead. I'm aware that He cares about my well-being because I care about His Kingdom. Since He cares, He leads. I have a partnership with God in which the course of my life and the agenda of His Kingdom are intertwined. My highest desire is to help expand the influence of the Kingdom. In this I feel I am aided, not by magical protection or mystical manipulation of events. No, God's help lies in His revealing the path which best leads to the expansion of His Kingdom and, therefore, to my own highest and best outcome.

Following God's leading is not greatly different from imagining what His Kingdom should be, and working to make that a reality. I envision a world in which the well-being of all people is a priority. That leads me to go in directions that will help bring that about. What does God want this world to become? The vision of that world is my guiding light.

The most difficult thing about loving God is not accepting God's leading. Oh, no—the really tough thing is being sure of what is God's leading and what is the misleading of my own selfishness or ignorance. The Scripture says, "There is a way that seems right to a person..." (Prov. 14:12; 16:25). Of course I want to follow God's direction and will, not my own selfish ambition. But how can I know for certain which is which? The voice of God in the night is very rare. Consider also that even with the pillar of cloud and fire to guide them the people, sadly, ended up in what seemed to be meaningless wandering in the wilderness for forty years. Even the clear beacon could not save them from their own faithlessness (Num. 14:33).

Still, one of the most important tests of loving the Lord completely is whether we're willing to trust Him without reservation—even into the wilderness. The crucial thing is to make a decision in our hearts and minds that we will go where He leads. Once this is decided, then every decision is confronted from that viewpoint. It makes a huge difference. We may not see the figurative pillar of cloud clearly or at all, but we're always looking for it—and just as importantly, going where we think it would be if we could see it.

Consider the difference. If we approach a situation with the determination to do what we think is best from our point of view, we are subject to the limitations of what is good for us. When we consciously apply the criteria of what is good for the Kingdom the horizon expands to include not only other people but also history, past and future. We are still forced to sort through the criteria, being aware of the distraction of self-interest, but our field of vision is so much larger than when we consider only what is best for ourselves.

God Becomes Real In the Following. Following God begins with believing that He does, in fact, lead. "Where are we going?" we ask. He responds, "To a place I will show you." It's an act of faith. It's one of the most important aspects of God being a reality, a Presence to us. When God truly exists for us, His direction and guidance are felt. When we accept that His leading is authentic,

He becomes present in the going, in the proceeding, in the moving ahead. Baruck, my Jewish friend on the flight to Frankfurt, said that "God must be real." God has been real to me in the leading—or more accurately, in my following.

Before she became a Supreme Court Justice, Sandra Day O'Connor and I were two of three judges at an American Legion speech contest. As we were becoming acquainted prior to the speeches she told me she had grown up in the Quaker tradition. I told her that one of the guiding principles of my life was a Quaker saying, "Proceed as the way opens." She was not acquainted with the saying.

After the contest was over she asked me to repeat the saying. I did, then added that I had modified it to fit my own experience— "Proceed AND the way opens." There is a subtle difference. "Proceed AS the way opens" assumes that the leading of God comes through the opening of doors, or perceptions, and especially opportunities. Sometimes that happens. We've all experienced it. An opening develops which seems clearly the leading of God. I have often experienced what I believe to be the leading of God in just that way.

"Proceed AND the way opens," my variation on the Quaker saying, acknowledges that there isn't always a clear or even foggy opening. One proceeds in faith anyway, believing that the sea will part as one steps into the water. The step comes before the parting.

I came to the place in my spiritual development that I wanted to test my beliefs outside my own sheltered community of faith. I had been nurtured by loving leaders who were devoted to serving God. They passed that devotion on to me. As my faith became informed with knowledge of Scripture, theology and history I began to sense a broader arena in which God was operating. I felt the nudge of God to step into my own limiting Red Sea. The barriers fell. My fears were put aside or ignored. I stepped into the abyss of the larger theological world. I stepped. The limiting sea parted.

I clearly understand that it was my desire to deepen my knowledge and faith that caused me to seek the opportunity to study in a different faith community. That desire, more than the letter of admission into the seminary, felt to me to be the leading of God. In a sense I created the opening by my action. I acted based on an inner need to expand my search for God. I proceeded AND the way opened.

The Wilderness of Waiting. There have been other times when I've been forced to make decisions where there was no clear opening. Out of those experiences I became aware of the necessity of waiting on God. Sometimes waiting is the only opening. I have found it to be true that "those who wait for the LORD shall renew their strength" (Isa. 40:31).

But we cannot stay in the waiting wilderness forever. At some point it's necessary to act with the assurance that a way will open. "Proceed AND the way opens." Sometimes the wall stands firm and a bloody nose is the result. More often the wall opens, or crumbles, sometimes differently from the expected, but an opening nevertheless. God's leading in those instances is not a pillar of cloud, but the simple assurance that He is WITH us.

From the beginning those who led the people of God listened for direction from God. They were tuned into God. I don't know how else to describe their gift, but it was real. It remains real. God led

Noah to build an ark. God led Abraham (first known as Abram, but referred to by his later name Abraham throughout this work) to a land that He showed him. Moses discovered the God of his fathers on Mt. Sinai, was directed to tell Pharaoh to let the people go and followed through by laying his life on the line.

It was Moses' not quite unfaltering following of God's leading that caused him to sing along with the people, "In Your unfailing love You will lead the people You have redeemed. In Your strength You will guide them to Your holy dwelling" (Ex. 15:13). God leads those who accept Him because He loves them. Moses affirms that God has the capacity and the desire to lead.

How were those great leaders led? God spoke to them, and we are told that they actually heard His voice, saw unexplainable manifestations of His power—blazing bushes that were not consumed, heard their names called in the middle of the night, were joined by a fourth man in the fire, and saw a pillar of smoke and fire going before them in the desert. They reported these and many other manifestations of God's leading. God led them by direct contact that they could not, or did not, mistake.

I have heard a good number of men and woman who have claimed that God talked to them and gave them directions. I must say that I always respond to these claims with enormous skepticism. It's not that I doubt that God could speak to anyone He chooses. There just have been too many instances in which my doubts in what they claimed to hear have proven correct.

I have never heard the voice of God, yet I can say that God has led me throughout my life. How can I say that? It isn't an exclusive or unique claim. I believe God offers guidance to every person who desires it and listens for it. I can't prove it. I can only recommend that people look for it and expect it. God's image is in every human being as a kind of internal "guidance system." That image is a resource for everyone who pays attention to it.

The Whisper of the Inner Spirit. God leads me through His Spirit, which is within every one of His children. This gift is promised at baptism, given when a person commits her life to God. There is God's Spirit within me. There is also distinct from God's Spirit, my spirit. Everyone who seeks the Spirit of God enjoys His Spirit along with her own spirit.

This view, of necessity, has both risk and opportunity. It's **risky** because it lends itself to selfish, narrow, and myopic claims. It provides **opportunity** by causing one to at least attempt to think and understand beyond herself...thinking in the Spirit.

What immediately comes to mind is some kind of inner voice or nudge in which a person hears or feels the direction of God. For me it is more like a whisper to which I must give my undivided attention if I am to understand correctly. In the movie, *The Ten Commandments*, Moses says of God, "I heard His voice in my head." This cannot, of course, be verified by another as presumably only the person being guided hears or feels. Again, great caution must be exercised as it's all too easy to superimpose our own inner voice over the voice of God. Such claims must always be verified by the community of God.

God leads in many ways. I think of Abraham who didn't have Scripture. God led him. How? Interestingly, the first step toward the place to which God called him was taken by his father, Terah.

We tend to connect with God only in the first person, but God is not thus limited. Abraham's call really came second handed through his father. It was nonetheless understood to be the call of God to Abraham (Heb. 11:8).

I wonder what religious history came to Abraham from his father? We have certain writings from Mesopotamia which could have been available to him—The *Epic of Gilgamesh*, for instance, which includes an account of a great flood. Obviously, the writings of Moses came after Abraham, but what religious stories and teachings did he grow up with? What caused him to feel the call of God to a distant land? We all have guiding works of literature and art in our history, sources from which we draw wisdom, inspiration and guidance. A part of what we love about God is the shared experience that ties our lives to those who have gone before and those who shall follow.

When a person does very well, whether in making a good decision, or an athletic performance, or avoiding a disaster, or other fortunate outcome, we say God was with him. Again, we must be careful in making such an assessment as sometimes in similar situations other Godly people may try as hard and have opposite outcomes. How can we say that God was with one of them and not the other? God can be with both of them and regardless of the outcome there is the confidence, as Joseph observed that, "God intended it for good" (Genesis 50:20).

Consulting the inner Spirit presents opportunity by giving freedom and boldness to take a course to which others may be blinded or where they may be fearful. It should never be an easy thing to say to a brother or sister that you disagree with what they perceive to be the direction of the Spirit. At the same time it is an obligation to say along with Peter, "we must obey God rather than men" (Acts 5:29).

How Can I Be Sure? I can't say I've always followed God's leading. I can say that I've always tried—I mean really been tuned into, and intentional in, following what I believe God wants me to do. Sure, that says God cares about what happens in my life. I believe that. I think everyone should believe that about themselves. At the same time I believe we need to be very cautious and humble in claiming that God led us in any particular instance. How could anyone be sure? Who besides Moses and the fleeing Israelites were guided by a pillar of cloud by day and a pillar of fire by night? Who besides Samuel and a few others can say they heard a voice in the night? Who besides Saul can say they saw a vision on the road to Damascus?

In Moses' case, and some others, the calling of God was not desired and was even resisted. God did the choosing. So far as we know, no one ever turned down the calling of God, though Moses tried and so did Jonah. Adam hid from God. Elijah was terrified by the earthquake, wind and fire. Jonah wasn't thrilled with his direct instructions from God. Saul, later known as the Apostle Paul, didn't welcome the words in the vision—but he followed them. God knows His woman and man, knows that they will respond because He knows their heart.

There is only the expectation and decision to be led—and the listening for the inner voice. I EXPECT God to lead me, and have since I was a boy. I didn't consult Him about mundane things like, which bike should I buy, or who should be my friends, or anything in which I felt I could make an intelligent choice on my own. I did ask for guidance about solving personal problems with friends, and difficulties at school. There was something about expecting that God would lead me that gave me a confidence that whatever I did, I was moving in the right direction.

There is a self-fulfilling element involved in expectation that might be seen as having nothing to do with God, but there also developed for me a reality of "Presence." I can't prove it—don't need to, as the process was functional for me. It worked. Asking God for wisdom as Solomon did was a self-fulfilling request. I must admit I'd like to prove it was real leading from God, but that simply isn't possible. I can recommend the approach based on my own experience—"Ask, and it will be given you" (Matt. 7:7).

It's not out of lack of confidence in my own analytical powers that I seek this Godly guidance. It's not from the uncertainty of facing the unknown that I look for direction from my heavenly Father. I simply sense that there is an internal compass, the nudge of God that feels very real—a whisper so real that I accept it as a sixth sense. I repeat, in this I do not feel that I have a special gift. I believe it's available to all who mind its "Presence."

Conflicts of the Spirit. The leading of the Spirit is available to all who seek Godly guidance, yet I must acknowledge that the leading seems sometimes inconsistent. Godly people do not always receive the same direction, even regarding the same decision. I don't know how to reconcile this apparent contradictory leading of the one Spirit. One explanation is that the Spirit of God and my own spirit are a team in which my own spirit may influence the Spirit of God where I am concerned. In another Godly person her spirit may influence the Spirit of God in a different direction that is also a Godly direction for her. In any situation it is likely that there is more than one path to a Godly goal.

Even Paul and Barnabas, both of whom had been set apart by the Holy Spirit for the same work (Acts 13:1, 2), later had a disagreement "so sharp that they parted company" (Acts 15:39). Barnabas went one direction and Paul another. The result was that instead of one mission occupying both, there were two missions with double the results. It's no easy matter to determine how or why the Spirit directs and how humans respond.

While I was wrestling with the decision in my own educational journey I faced encouragement from one esteemed professor, Richard Phillips whom I've already mentioned, and opposition from another. Dr. Phillips was very aware of the turmoil in my spirit as I tried to reconcile the God with whom I had grown up and the God with whom I was now struggling. He suggested that I might wish to look at other seminaries where my questions would not be unwelcome. While he was open to any question, no matter how outrageous, the seminary was not open to my difficult questions about God.

The Seminary to which I had applied had asked for a letter from the dean of the Seminary stating that I was in good standing. I asked the dean if he would write the letter. With a grave look he said, "I'll write it, but I hope they don't take you. They'll rob you of your fire." I held my tongue, but wanted to say, "My own rigid and legalistic approach to Scripture that has developed here in this place is draining my spirit and putting out the fire of my own passion for bringing the lost to Christ. I want to go to a place where perhaps adversarial winds might fan into flame the spark that is dying." I felt certain I was following the leading of God for me even though it felt I was being led into a storm.

I believe the dean felt he was being led by God to discourage me from going to a place that he feared would destroy my faith. He was correct in understanding that I was doing a risky thing. He was a good man, a Godly man, and had made a positive impression on my life.

I think highly of him still. Yet in retrospect, I can say he was mistaken in discouraging me from following a path that was necessary for me. He could not see my heart, and I think would have been incapable of understanding where I was with God at that moment. I knew I would have been incapable of explaining it. He was one of my teachers. I rejected his leading. How could I do that? How could I be sure God was leading me and not him?

There comes a time when every person must look within and attempt to determine whether their resistance to another's view of God's will is based on flawed personal vision or sincere response to the Spirit of God within. Again, I believe that the foundational test must be Scripture—BUT, the words of God are not written only on paper. They are also written upon the heart (Rom. 2:15; II Cor. 3:2,3; Heb. 8:10, 10:16; *et al.*). My spirit made the judgment that the dean was being guided by his own understanding, the narrowness of which was strangling my spirit. His approach to God and Scripture was killing my love for God.

I believe that God, through a Godly mentor, led me in taking the educational path I took. I'm pretty sure I wouldn't have found it by myself. I believe that God led me in meeting and marrying my wife. I believe God led me in moving to Arizona. I believe God led me in starting a new Church. I believe God led me during the years I served Him in that Church. In these crucial events in my life I looked for God's leading. I found it.

When I say I have felt the leading of the Spirit in my life I say it with the greatest humility. I do not claim that my version of the leading of the Spirit has always been correct. I don't know. I do know that in virtually every decision I've made, in my own life and in leading God's Church, my decisions have been based on what I have felt to be a response to God's Spirit within—God's leading. When I've consciously looked for that leading I have never been disappointed with the outcome.

God Is My Partner. Following seminary I was offered a position with a Church in New Jersey where I was serving as youth minister while in seminary. The community was beautiful and in some ways idyllic. I had built a strong ministry with the youth of the Church and had become close to many families. The Senior Minister of many years was retiring and the Church leaders asked me to consider taking the position.

While I was being considered for that position, I was contacted by a Church across the country in Arizona inviting me to interview for a position as an Associate Minister. I told them I was pretty certain I'd be staying at the Church where I was. They were insistent, adding that even if I wasn't interested, at least let them fly my wife and me out for a visit. I agreed and we had a most agreeable visit. The visit resulted in an offer from that Church as well as the one in New Jersey, so now I was faced with two offers. Which position was the one where God wanted me?

The decision should have been easy. The scale was heavily weighted on the side of staying in New Jersey. We knew and loved the people there. We'd been treated kindly, even magnanimously. The position was for Senior Minister, and at twenty-eight years of age I felt I had waited long enough for that level of responsibility.

The last night before the day I had promised the churches a decision I sat at the kitchen table as midnight approached. I felt the confidence that whatever decision I made, God would be in it. At the same time I searched my soul for tiny nuances that were at work within me. There was a large difference in salaries. We were settled where we were. Both had great, but different, opportunities. My wife and I had discussed both situations thoroughly. She assured me she would be supportive of whichever decision I made.

I sensed that this was an important crossroad. There were good things about each offer, but how could we walk away from a more attractive financial offer and the position of Senior Minister? For two hours I wrestled with God, mostly in prayer, some within my own heart and mind. Almost every factor in the decision pointed toward staying in New Jersey. The facts said stay where I was. Why was I so hesitant to accept the obvious choice? Why indeed? I earnestly prayed, sensing that this was a crucial decision of my life, of our lives.

It was a great dilemma for me and led to a new understanding of God's leading. Is it possible that God gives us choices, all of which are embraced by His leading? As I confronted the two opportunities I felt the tension of wanting to make the Godly choice. I also felt a developing peace that God would be in, and honor, whichever choice I made. I prayed, I reasoned, I sought counsel and then I pushed myself to a moment of encounter. It was an encounter with God, with my self, and with the moment. Somewhere in the encounter emerged a certainty—not a voice or a sign—an awareness that Arizona was my "promised land."

Different Roads Can Both Be Right. I believe, *Ex eventu,* the move to Arizona was the best, the most expanding, the most productive and creative decision I could have made. At the same time I feel certain that if I had stayed in New Jersey I would have had a very satisfying ministry. I can never know for certain, except that it gave me the certainty that in the future, whatever path I chose, God would be with me. I love the road I took in Arizona, and would not trade it for any I can imagine. I learned to trust God more through this whole process. I can say I learned to love Him through trust—AND through following!

Looking back it still seems illogical that I left New Jersey. It wasn't the last illogical thing I did. I ministered happily with the Church in Phoenix for over eight years. I loved the people; I got along well with the Senior Minister; I had a salary equal to what I had been offered eight years before in New Jersey, and was the heir apparent to the "throne" of being the next Senior Minister. The Senior Minister asked if I would prepare to follow him in a few years. We began to actively move toward that goal and I assumed greater responsibilities of leadership.

One day the Senior Minister asked if I'd like to do a backyard wedding far out in a remote part of the desert. I've always enjoyed these events, so I agreed. I believe it was in May of 1977 that the wedding occurred. I drove the desert roads out into the boondocks. The main road was a two-lane blacktop with no center line. I turned off that road onto a gravel road, and a few miles later into a little isolated neighborhood that was surrounded by hundreds of square miles of wide open spaces. There was gorgeous desert for about as far as the eye could see.

I performed the wedding, and enjoyed a bit of refreshment after we signed the license, then started the long journey home. I had noticed little pockets of dwellings here and there on the way to the wedding, but hadn't paid much attention. I'd hiked in that area, taken the youth group camping nearby, and driven through it several times on my way to the lake that was beyond it. It occurred to me that there would soon be a lot of houses out there.

When I arrived home I said to my wife, "Someone ought to start a new church out there." It was some sixteen miles from the Church where I ministered, and the closest other church in our brotherhood was about ten miles from the location of the wedding. Our brotherhood had a new church planting agency, and I mentioned the region to the director. He told me that it was one of the areas he had been looking at.

The summer passed and I couldn't get the thought out of my mind. "Someone needs to start a new church out there." I truly didn't have myself in mind. Why would I? My future was set, tied up with a nice ribbon. I would think about starting a new church at night. It would be in my mind when I woke up. I daydreamed about it. "Somebody...." I have no recollection of when or in what form, "Somebody should start a new church..." became "I should start a new church...."

I had not prayed about it because it simply was not what I perceived as an option for me. It would be going against the leading of God to even think about leaving the place to which He had called me. I had a strong sense that God had brought me to the Church in Phoenix, and every indication was that He wanted me to stay there to continue the finest ministry of which I had ever been a part.

The Un-Welcomed Different Road. What happened is an example of how I think God works in our lives even when we're content with where we are. It's called complacency. Why would we want to change anything when all is well? My vision was too narrow to imagine that there was an alternative to the "cherry" position I had been offered. The very fact that the promotion had been offered was confirmation that I was where God wanted me, or so I reasoned. Everyone took it for granted and began to act as though I would be the next Senior Minister. I believe that God does His most important directing when we aren't aware that we need directing.

I loved the road I was on and looked forward to the years of ministry that lay before me with opportunities I hadn't imagined. I wasn't looking for a different road. I didn't welcome a different road! Yet, the different road would not be denied. I would say, God would not be denied.

One morning I said to my wife, I think God wants me to start a new Church out in north Scottsdale. I believe she said something like, "But what about the position here where we are?" "I know," I replied, "but I just can't get it out of my mind." We talked about it and I sensed that not only was she open to the idea but that she felt it was the best thing for me to do. From that time on she was totally encouraging of my exploring the possibility. I would need that encouragement.

I didn't say anything immediately to the leadership of the Church. I wasn't sure yet. This might just be a wild hare, a whim, or a passing fancy. I did begin to pray about it, in earnest. This was crazy. It didn't make sense. What could I be thinking? But the idea was there and it wouldn't let go of me. For days I wrestled with the thought. There was no moment I can remember, no "come to Jesus meeting" with myself as had occurred at the previous Church. I just gradually became convinced that God was calling me to start that new Church.

Did I say, "convinced?" Sometimes yes. Sometimes no. The second-guessing that went on from there was tortuous. I'd go to bed with the thought, "I think God is calling me to do this." I'd wake up with the terrifying—really, terrifying!—thought, "What are you thinking?"

This was my first experience with the concept that "God gives the idea to the person He wishes to do it." That has guided me ever since. Mustering my courage I said to the Senior Minister, "I think God is calling me to start a new Church in north Scottsdale." "Let us help you," he said. `

I didn't hear a voice in my head saying, "Larry, start a new church." I had resisted the very notion of it. Even though I felt "called by God"—I don't know how else to express it—the call was not crystal clear, or was it? Against all my doubts and fears about it I moved ahead and announced a starting date for the new Church. From the day of its beginning there remained in my mind some doubt, but determination overcame the doubt—"Proceed, and the way opens." If it had indeed been other than a real call from God, I knew it had great potential for good, and I was determined to prove—to myself if no other—that God was in it. That was certainly to be put to the test.

Peaches and Cream Followed by Bread and Water. All was peaches and cream for the first year—mostly. We had good numbers for a new Church, our finances were okay—a few lean weeks, but that was to be expected. Our attendance was good—sixty to eighty souls usually, including children. New people came to us rapidly enough to replace those who moved or fell by the wayside. By the end of the first year we were meeting our goals.

The second year was not so good. The honeymoon was over, as they say. Some Sundays we had less than fifty people. They were generous people, and great leaders, but the "grand opening halo" was gone. It was tough. I called in the homes of people who visited. Every single person who visited our worship services got a visit from me. I called on any "suspect" whose name was given to me. It was tough sledding—a bad but apt metaphor, for the desert. I began to grow discouraged. If God had called me to start a new Church, why wasn't it growing? We were providing classes for children, excellent music, preaching as good as I could do, contacts in the community through participation in civic life, expensive advertising in the newspaper—everything I could think of to get people involved.

A few of my visits were positive, at least enough to replace the people who were leaving, but we were not growing. The most frequent response I would get from visitors was, "We're looking for a church that has a building. We'll think about it when you have a building." One dark night after four or five such refusals I was driving home as dejected as I had ever been since launching the Church. Driving down through the desolate and deserted road known as Dreamy Draw I remember clearly praying to God, "Oh God. Oh God." I wasn't swearing. I was simply calling out to God. Then I asked myself, "Whatever made you think you could start a new Church?"

I didn't hear an audible voice. There were no shooting stars or other visual manifestations of a "Presence." But I know the words formed clearly and decisively in my mind—"Larry, you aren't starting it. I am."

I can't prove it was God speaking, but it made the difference. I stopped thinking of what I was doing to start the Church. If God wanted it to be a success, He would have to do what I couldn't. And He did.

I have applied that view to every time of discouragement I've faced since. "God, if you want this to happen, you're going to have to do it." Does that then cause God to do something objective, or does it create a positive response in my attitude that fosters success? I can't say for sure. I can say for sure that it has worked. I can say as a result, I know what it is to have God WITH me.

Sanctified Uncertainty. Here is where my present understanding of what it means to love God saves me from self-doubt or recrimination in my own decisions. How do I know that any of my decisions were or are the correct ones? It's possible I made wrong choices one hundred percent of the time. It's also possible that every choice did reflect the will of God. I simply can't know. The best part is, I don't need to know. I trust the God I love to provide what is necessary to carry out His will, His purpose.

Martin Luther has been quoted as saying, "Love God and sin boldly!" No, Luther was not condoning sin. He was condoning mistakes made in good conscience. No one can ever be completely certain that a decision is the best decision. Who even knows for sure what "best" is? Only God knows.

Sometimes when I consult God about a matter it seems the answer I receive is, "You choose. Either path will please me. Both paths have interesting but different possibilities." I think God takes pleasure in letting us work through the maze of expanding opportunities on our own. The important thing is that if you love God, you are free to act boldly. Why?

Simple. "We know that in everything God works for good with those who love Him... (Rom. 8:28, RSV). I've always lived by that view of my relationship with God. Sometimes we wander in the wilderness for what seems forever. Is that God's will? Not necessarily, but maybe. The view of Scripture is that God punished the people with forty years in the desert because of their lack of faith. What if they had demonstrated great faith at the beginning? Who knows if they would have been successful in entering the land? They may not have been ready. We simply can't see every possibility. Maybe the desert wandering was necessary in order to prepare them for things for which they weren't yet ready.

If my eyes are on God and I miss something, which is inevitable, it isn't "game over." It's a variation on the game, offering a different route that might have an even better outcome. To love God is, at the very least, to accept what happens as good because it happens WITH God. God does not abandon us, even in the wilderness of our own making. In fact, I believe He uses the wilderness for our good. He leads even in the wilderness.

I trust God to lead me because I believe He loves me. If He truly loves me, He will not leave me to wander aimlessly. I believe His promise to men and women of old—"I am with you." Just how He is with me I can't explain. I simply believe it. What I can explain is that I desire to love Him fully in return and that causes me to look for His leading.

IV.
God of All Ages

As the Scriptures say, God does not change (Mal. 3:6). He has been known to change His mind—ask Lot or Abraham or even Hosea. But God Himself changing? No. He is Who He is.

So where do all of the different personalities attributed to God come from? We all read the same Bible, seeing how God relates to His people and the world down through the ages. Yet people come to different conclusions about what God is like.

In his book, *Your God Is Too Small,* J. B. Phillips describes the different personalities people ascribe to God. There is God as the policeman, the parent, the grand old man, the God in a box, and others. Jesus settles pretty much on one image...Father.

Most of us relate all too well with Mr. Phillips' descriptions of the way people see God. In fact, if we are honest we will probably acknowledge that we ourselves have attributed different personalities to God at different stages of our lives. I have understood God in at least nine different roles during my own lifetime. With thanks to Mr. Phillips I offer my own stages of how I understood God.

Super Angel. When I first became aware of God as a little boy I understood Him as a kind of super angel...someone Who watched over me, protected me, guided me, assisted me, and best of all, the

One Who gave me wonderful parents and this world. This was the "Jesus loves me, This I know" God, and I prayed to Him beside my bed most nights before going to bed.

I enjoyed thinking about God, praying to Him, knowing He sent the birds and flowers, and potatoes and watermelons, and especially popcorn just for my enjoyment. God and I were good friends. He was able to do miracles like making me well when I was sick. My favorite stories were of Samuel hearing God call him in the night, David slaying a giant with a sling, and Jesus walking on the water.

Policeman. I wasn't very old when I began to think of God as somewhat fearsome, the truant officer Who watched my every move with a less than benevolent eye. He punished little boys and girls who told lies, or who were mean to their brothers and sisters, or didn't obey their parents, or missed going to church. He wasn't exactly unkind, but He was very strict about the rules. He didn't cut a fellow much slack.

I was afraid of God and the punishment of hell. It wasn't that He was mean or unfair. A kid just couldn't get away from Him and it was very easy to do something without thinking, like breaking a window while playing, or complaining about having to do dishes or cleaning up my room. I tried my best to be good, but always knew I didn't quite meet His standards.

This policeman God was not my friend. He still watched over me, but more to be a critic than to make sure I got the most out of the world. In Sunday school classes I learned that God punishes children who step out of line. The Bible stories that made an impression on me were Adam and Eve eating the apple, David doing something bad with

Bathsheba, and Judas betraying Jesus. Dad still read the Bible stories to us and "Daniel in the Lions' Den" was my favorite. God still protected His children, but Daniel was a better man than I could ever be.

General of the Universe. The next image I had of God was of the general in the sky Who was waiting for just the right moment to send His Son back on the clouds of the sky to straighten things out. This cloud-conquering prince would gather everybody together and bring us before God Who would hand down the verdict. It wasn't going to be a pretty sight. I hoped somehow I'd squeak by.

The images I had of Jesus suddenly appearing at the moment I least expected were terrifying. I had nightmares of this world-ending event when everything I cherished in life came to a horrifying end. I still prayed to God but more to keep on good terms than to visit with Him or even to ask Him for things I wanted. I asked Him to forgive me a lot. "Forgive me for all my sins," was a frequent prayer. I often couldn't think of many specific sins, but I knew He kept track of every one.

I read enough of Revelation to develop strong images of what the end of the world was going to be like. Hell and damnation weren't frequent topics in the sermons I heard, but God's punishment for sin was almost always mentioned. When an evangelist would preach on the second coming I would have nightmares for weeks.

I read the Bible a lot because I wanted to know what was expected of me. I began to develop a pretty clear picture of what God's rules were and what was important to Him. The most important thing to Him I began to realize was to accept Him and worship Him in the way He said. I knew the right ways. They were the ways I had been taught.

My little church in Tower Hill, Illinois had the correct formula figured out. You became a Christian by confessing your belief in Jesus as the Son of God, by being baptized—only complete immersion counted—and living the Christian life. Living the Christian life pretty much consisted of going to church every Sunday—morning and night, and tithing. If I earned three dollars mowing a yard, thirty cents went into the offering. Wednesday night prayer meeting was required of adults, but children had school work to do, so they didn't have to go until they grew up.

Supreme Judge. At this stage of my faith I would say that God was like a judge and thankfully I was His spokesperson. I knew what He expected of my friends, and I wasn't hesitant to tell them. It was during this time that I realized that God wanted me to be a preacher. He wanted me to warn everyone of the judgment that was in store for them if they didn't follow His rules.

God for me was less fearsome by this time. He took no pleasure in sending people to hell. He was simply being just and fair. He had made His rules very clear and if people ignored them or understood them incorrectly there was no excuse. For Him to make exceptions, unfortunately wouldn't be right or possible, or so I concluded.

This view of God wasn't solely my own invention, but it suited me well. Preachers and Bible school leaders and camp counselors reinforced this understanding of God. It made sense to me and I couldn't understand how others could be so blind to the truth.

Passages of Scripture more than the stories shaped my relationship with God at this stage. "For God so loved the world that He gave His only begotten Son, that whoever believes in Him should not perish, but have everlasting life" (Jn. 3:16), was my favorite. So simple was this statement, and so clear that if one did not believe, they would perish.

What did "believe" mean to me? Exactly what Jesus and the apostles taught—exactly as I understood it. On the day of Pentecost after hearing Peter's sermon the people asked, "What must we do to be saved?" Peter's response said it all—"Repent and be baptized every one of you for the forgiveness of your sins" (Acts 2:38). What could be clearer than that?

A moment of reflection allows me to acknowledge that I still believe what the Scriptures teach about these things. What bothers me about my view of God as Supreme Judge is the dogmatic attitude it reflected in my own life. I loved algebra and science. The formulas and rules were very precise and unbending. That fit my understanding of, and relationship with, God.

So was this legalistic view of God a part of my discovery and assimilation of the precision of math and laws of science? Was this dealing with God a part of my mental development? I believe it was, and that it fit into the way my brain was developing. It just missed my heart—and soul. I loved people—loved them enough to decide I would devote my life to saving them from hell. Oh my, how devoted I was to being God's messenger of salvation, as well as his court judge handing down the verdict. I had a lot to learn.

King. God as Judge gradually evolved into God as King. He owned the whole realm and passed down royal decrees. He had called me to be one of His messengers. My task was to tell the whole world what the King expected and call on them to obey. It was with this understanding that I went off to Bible College. There, most of my views of the King's rules were reinforced and solidified.

By the time I was twenty-one I knew I had been privileged with the truth about God. My mission in life was to bring everyone who was willing to this correct view of what God required. I was confident, sometimes brash, and always certain that I had spoken with the blessing of the King.

I reflect on these changing understandings of God because I think it necessary if I am to understand what it means to love God, to know how I understood God, and how I now understand Him. Who is this God that I am attempting to love with all my heart, soul, mind and strength? How can I love Him unless I know him?

My changing views of God happened gradually and naturally, but not without difficulty. The God Who was my childhood friend resisted giving away to the policeman God—the end of a beautiful friendship. The Policeman God was less threatening than the General in the Sky Who would one day destroy all things. It was easier to get along with the Judge, because rules suited me. At least I knew what was expected.

Seeing God as The King allowed me to transfer my concern for my own eternal destination, to a great compassion for all the lost people of the world. I was a confidant of the King, sat at His table, and even fancied myself his advisor from time to time. God and I were not necessarily at peace. I just knew where I stood with Him. Loving Him was not my goal. I was His messenger and servant. It was enough that He had sent me on His mission to save the world.

I was eager to get out in the world and preach the good news. Never mind that sometimes it was bad news for those who thought they were all right with God. It was my unpleasant, but necessary, duty to inform them otherwise if they didn't have it right. I saw myself as preaching the truth and people coming to hear me in order to escape the judgment that was to come.

Dark Knight. Then the King, as I understood him, betrayed me. It wasn't that God betrayed me. My "carved in stone" idea of God betrayed me. His rules, which I knew so well and had defended for a decade, no longer seemed fair. A dread feeling of uncertainty crept into my mind…into my soul. I had been so certain, so sure of my understanding of what God expected. When I was confronted with the reality that my dogmatic spirit was the result of an underlying insecurity about my beliefs it hit me like a freight train. Highballing along the straight and certain track, it was as though the track suddenly evaporated before my eyes.

It was a moment of revelation for me. In an instant I knew there were huge flaws in the limitations I had placed on God. There had been some nagging suspicions from time to time but I'd always been able to fight them down. Not this time. In a matter of a very few days I realized I was in an impossible position. The falling apart of my concept of God was almost physically painful. It left me in a devastating mental anguish.

I faced an impossible dilemma. If God saved those who had a different understanding of the rules than mine, it wouldn't be fair to those of us who had worked so hard to do it just the way He said. If He sent them to hell because they hadn't gotten the word, or had been taught incorrectly, that seemed unloving and unfair. Either way, it didn't fit the God I thought I knew. How could God on the one hand reveal His truth only to us fortunate few, yet on the other hand send ignorant and often well-meaning people to hell?

I had no choice. I knew I had to confront God and get an explanation. Enrolling in an independent multi-denominational seminary was a way to confront my own inner conflicts. I would either regain my confidence in my own certain view of God, or discover the truth that I had been wrong. I had demonized the professors of these liberal seminaries and saw them as enemies in the faith. Now I looked to them to help me discover a larger view of God.

There came the darkness of separating myself from a God Who didn't make sense, a God I no longer understood. I didn't give up on Him, but He had become a dark mystery to me, and a disappointment. He had His rules, but His rules as I had understood them could not fully fit the human situation.

For three years I struggled and wrestled with God. At times I reverted to my former certainty that I knew God's truth. The battle raged within me. How could I give up my cherished rules? At other times I gave up on Him, feeling it just wasn't possible to come to terms with Him and it wasn't worth the effort. I felt a huge inner struggle to get my mind around a God Who loved and accepted beyond my own capacity to love and accept. My concept of God had been shattered. The pieces just didn't fit together anymore.

I was surrounded by mostly sympathetic and helpful fellow students, many who were themselves searching for a workable understanding of God in the world. Professors were heroic in their faith in this God Who was so difficult to pin down. I descended into a great darkness in which I despaired of loving life ever again. I didn't hate God but I must say that I blamed my pain on Him and felt He was responsible for my being misled—and miserable. I expected never to be at peace again.

The Phoenix. I don't know how it happened, or when, but from the ashes of the God Who had crumbled before me began to emerge a new image of God, a Phoenix. I didn't need to pin Him down on every detail of His truth or nature. It was enough to believe that He was there—had been there all along—and that we could still talk to each other.

The sense of betrayal gave way to a realization that I had all along been trying to make God in my own image. God simply wouldn't have any part in it. I had to accept His unknowable-ness as an ongoing quest for a relationship between being and Spirit. There emerged an uneasy reconciliation in which I desired only that God lead me and instruct me.

Professor, Counselor, Lord. Thus it has been for some forty years...God the professor, sometimes the counselor, always the One to Whom I've turned for guidance in my life. When I've spoken of Him and on His behalf it's always been with a sense of attempting to encourage people in their own walk with Him and urging them to engage in their own struggle. I do not regret my own time of turmoil. In fact, I treasure it.

When I was a kid I would wrestle with my brother, who was two years younger than I. He was stronger than I, but I was more agile. It was an interesting and developmental exercise of the body that I think benefited us both. That is how I think of my wrestling with God these years. He has increased my spiritual awareness of the world and left me with a sense of awe and wonder about this great mystery we call human life.

Now, after a satisfying career in being God's messenger I feel the wrestling, though not over, has reached a stage of reflection. I have experienced God in great times and in terrible, in good times and bad, in happy and sad events. The confrontation was more with the events than with God. I struggled in trying to understand them and to learn from them, and to share whatever I learned with others if they wanted to hear.

Companion and Friend. The struggle has brought me to a place of companionship with God. God is my friend again, more like the first God I knew than any of the others. Strange that I can now say of God almost the exact things I said of my first image...except I don't see Him as a Super Angel but as my Friend. He watches over me, guides me, assists me and best of all gives me this world to enjoy and family and friends with whom to share it.

Notice I left out "protects me" for I think He does what a Spirit can to protect all His children and creatures. He expects us to look out for ourselves and for one another. His protection is not so much for this life as for eternal life. Jesus' love for God has led me to my own love for God, so my song has become "God of our Fathers, Whose almighty hand, leads forth in beauty all the starry band...."

Talking to God has become more a continual communion than events of prayer. I pray when something is heavy on my mind that needs special attention, and when leading others in listening to God out loud. I love knowing He created all the earth for my enjoyment—and His. I didn't expect Him to do miracles, but He has certainly performed wonders and shaped my life. Yes, as I think about what God has done in the years I've walked with Him, He did miracles.

Life for me has been a continuing discovery of the human experience, beginning with loving parents. Discovery continued through study of the Bible and other holy writings, and with a host of teachers, friends and even enemies. God has shaped me through them all—every one. I still walk in the woods and look for mushrooms. I gaze and wonder at the night sky, marveling at the God beyond it all. I've walked a fair part of the world, which for me has been better than walking on water. I have slain no giants, but have tamed a few. I've taken care of people, and as often received their care.

I've known the blessing and luxury of being a partner to the wife I love. Surpassing me, she has helped me surpass myself. Children have taught me what it means for a father to be loved. I've known the love of a great Church and see God in its embracing love and service.

I began this chapter with the objective of understanding how differently God can appear at different stages of life. I hope that each person reading this will look back on their own life and see how their concept of God has grown. Most importantly, I hope that each person will engage in the struggle to know and love God, and in the process to make Him their Friend.

Resolution. At first I thought of these changing views of God as simply erroneous thinking that should have been corrected at once. The dogmatic and narrow views I once had of God still cause me to wince, and I am embarrassed at certain memories of acting badly in dealing with people who thought differently from me. Upon thinking about my mental and psychological development I've not only come to peace with the various stages, I am thankful for them.

Each stage allowed me to think about God in a different way, such that my present understanding of God is, I believe, much broader and richer than it would have been had I come to a more mature view of God earlier. God as Supreme Judge gave me a passion for saving people from the punishment, not only of hell, but also the natural consequences that result from wrong actions. God as King still gives me a feeling of satisfaction and responsibility that I speak on behalf of His Majesty.

I believe my passion for saving lost people grows out of my childhood fear of the dread consequences of Christ's second coming. This image of the end of time gave me a sense of the urgency of life, and the importance of preaching the gospel. I felt it in the deep recesses of my own insecurity about the outcome of my own life. For whatever reason, I projected this concern for my own well-being onto other people. At first it was the insecurity, I believe, of needing to convince others in order to convince myself. Happily it has expanded to embrace the understanding that the God Who fills the whole universe is most beautifully seen in my own being, and in the beings around me

PART II
Life Through The Eyes Of God

V.
Loving God's Work

God's Goalie. There are worse situations than being caught between a rock and a hard place. At least both opponents are benign. How much worse to be caught between an angry bull and a rabid dog? Or between a wolf and a bear? A friend described an attack from two directions in a new way. Speaking of his role in trying to help his son and daughter-in-law through marital problems he wrote: "I personally did everything I could to hold on to both sides, but it's a poor position to play 'goalie' and let both sides slap pucks at you."

He continued, "I love God with all my heart, mind and soul. I love God's work over all other work, and love His people with passion and fervor. Sometimes I don't love their behavior, and I know the old Evil One is slithering around on this earth to toss those pucks at us."

This man is a highly successful businessman who, while involved in the Church most of his life, has spent his career in a variety of businesses. Yet he says, **"I love God's work over all other work."** It isn't that he necessarily saw his businesses as God's work, but that he did God's work while he ran his businesses. What, after all, is the "work of God?"

How we perceive the work of God says a lot about our view of God. There are people in this world who perceive the work of God to include flying airplanes into the world trade center or, blowing themselves and others up in the middle of a crowded marketplace. There are also those of us who believe the work of God is to try to show those who are filled with such hatred that God loves everyone, both them and us.

My "goalie" friend later stated that, "the highest (and hardest) of God's work is to love the unlovable. That's way harder than loving my brother. To love the hostile, unreasonable and disagreeable people—those whose values and goals are totally different from my own is hard work. We have to force ourselves, but we know God loves them, so if we love God, we must love what God loves."

Then his thoughts took a turn that I had not connected with this concept of loving any who might be difficult to love. "If I am to love God, I must love myself just as I am, for God does. If I am to love others in whom I find weakness, flaws, hatred and evil, I must love myself as well. That also is a part of the work of God."

To love what God loves in others is one of the highest forms of loving God. I once knew a woman who had a unique perspective on this. She said, "When I meet a person I don't care for I say to myself, 'God loves that person and I intend to find out why!'"

We have all met people who challenge our ability to love. My friend intimated that sometimes he himself was that person that he felt it difficult to love. The beautiful possibility is that when we truly love God we are freed from hatred, for self or any other person. While we, along with Paul, feel wretched for the evil we see within ourselves or others, we choose not to hate, but to love. We humbly exclaim along with Paul, "Thanks be to God through Jesus Christ our Lord!" (Rom. 7:15-25).

Jesus said, "And I, when I am lifted up from the earth, will draw all people to myself" (Jn. 12:32). That includes every person who ever walked on this earth. No one is beyond the love of God. Doing His work means loving others as He loves them. Showing compassion to hurting, angry, hateful, lost and frightened people is definitely the work of God. Embracing His compassion for others and for ourselves is one of the most liberating ways in which we love Him.

The Work of God in the Three Abrahamic Religions. It is work, the actual activity of producing something of benefit to ourselves and to others that I wish to connect with what it means to love God. It would be easy to associate the work of God only with what we would call religious activity. That is not what is represented in any of the three Abrahamic religions, as I understand them. Those doing religious work are seen as doing the work of God, but they don't have an "exclusive" on His work.

JUDAISM. In Judaism the just and merciful treatment of all people by other people is clearly understood to be the work of God. In fact, acting justly and loving mercy is valued above sacrifices, the traditional work of the priests. The prophet Micah writes:

> He has told you, O mortal, what is good; and what does the LORD require of you but to do justice, and to love kindness, and to walk humbly with your God? The voice of the Lord cries to the city.... Can I tolerate wicked scales and a bag of dishonest weights? (Micah 6:8-11)

The work of God as described by Micah includes virtually every interaction among people. It goes beyond mere justice and calls for "kindness." I understand kindness as refraining from responding according to what another deserves but treating them better than they deserve. This is the concept involved in loving the unlovable. It's the work of God because it requires kindness.

ISLAM. Islam is often misunderstood, both by those looking at it from the outside and sometimes apparently by some who profess to practice it. Many people believe that Muslims understand the work of God as including doing violence to those who oppose or criticize Islam. There are some Muslims who do see the destruction of non-Muslims as being the work of God. That is absolutely not taught in the Koran. In fact, I think most would agree after examining the texts that the Koran is at least as kind toward non-Muslims as the Old Testament is toward non-Jews.

With regard to other believers the prophet Muhammad writes, "Surely God enjoins the doing of justice and the doing of good (to others) and the giving to the kindred…" (The Bee, 16:90). Again he writes, "If two parties of the believers quarrel, make peace between them…with justice and act equitably; surely God loves those who act equitably (The Chambers, 49:9). This reflects a very similar view of the work of God as we have seen in Judaism, including God's love for those who act to make peace.

Even more to the point with regard to non-Muslims Muhammad writes,

> It may be that God will bring about friendship between you and those whom you hold to be your enemies among them; and God

is Powerful; and God is Forgiving, Merciful. God does not forbid you respecting those who have not made war against you on account of (your) religion, and have not driven you forth from your homes, that you show them kindness and deal with them justly; surely God loves the doers of justice. (The Examined One 60:7, 8)

To "show them kindness and deal with them justly" extends the forgiveness of God to those who treat non-Muslims in this favorable manner. However, the same passage continues,

God only forbids you respecting those who made war upon you on account of (your) religion, and drove you forth from your homes and backed up (others) in your expulsion, that you make friends with them, and whoever makes friends with them, these are the unjust. (The Examined One, 60:9)

Note that Muhammad states that Muslims are forbidden to make friends with "those who made war upon you on account of your religion, and drove you forth from your homes...." Even so, "It may be that God will bring about friendship between you and those whom you hold to be your enemies among them." The writer bases this on the characteristics of God, Who is "Forgiving, Merciful." This passage clearly does not call for violent acts against even those "you hold to be your enemies." Yet sadly, some adherents to Islam have interpreted it as condoning violence.

I am not defending in any way the attacks by Muslim terrorists on anyone else. Even their own holy writings do not see those attacks as the work of God. Islam has ninety-nine names for God, including the Kind, the Generous, the Merciful, and the Forgiving. None of His names suggest vengeance or violence.

CHRISTIANITY. The followers of Jesus are expressly forbidden from retaliating, even against those who attack or oppose them. In fact, Jesus commanded His followers to love their enemies, and more.

> But I tell you who hear Me: Love your enemies, do good to those who hate you, bless those who curse you, pray for those who mistreat you. If someone strikes you on one cheek, turn to him the other also. If someone takes your cloak, do not stop him from taking your tunic. Give to everyone who asks you, and if anyone takes what belongs to you, do not demand it back. Do to others as you would have them do to you. (Lk. 6:27-31)

This passage is filled with seemingly unreasonable and even inappropriate actions. Love your enemies. Bless those who curse you. Turn the other cheek. Lend without expecting repayment. Those who first heard those words must have thought, "Surely you're joking! That doesn't make any sense at all." But it came to be the defining theme in all that Jesus taught, and is summed up in the last sentence of that passage, "Be merciful, just as your Father is merciful" (Luke 6:36).

Jesus was talking to individuals, though what He says could easily be extended to apply to the behavior of nations. Has any nation ever attempted to conduct their national affairs in this way? Would it work in international relations, or would it end up turning land and wealth over to those willing to be the most brutal?

That is a subject for another time but it does raise a larger issue that is troubling. If the work of God includes aiding those who are treated unjustly, at what point does this extend to intervening in one's neighbors' unjust actions toward innocent victims? To what extent does it apply to military intervention in other nations where injustice is evident?

The extent to which this approach applies to national relations is problematic for a number of reasons. First of all the United States is not a theocracy. Our constitution and laws are not based strictly on Christianity. To apply all of Christian teaching to how our nation conducts its affairs would not be acceptable to our non-Christian citizens. Just as significantly, it would also result in conflicts among Christians due to their own differences among themselves.

Beyond the internal diversity of religious behavior, there is the complexity of the world community, the majority of which does not follow the Christian religion. The early Church lived in a much smaller arena in which the clash of cultures, while present, was somewhat mitigated by Roman civilization, the *Pax Romana,* which imposed its own civil law. Jesus did not directly address an approach to international relations.

This is not to say that our understanding of loving God doesn't apply to international relations. It most certainly does. In the matter, for instance, of our intervention in Bosnia, the answer to the question, "What would Jesus do?" is not easy. The supposedly Christian Serbs and Croats were systematically assaulting, even murdering, the Muslim Bosniaks. The United States led the effort to forcefully end this violence. Was that a Christian thing to do?

On an individual level, if a Christian were to observe a neighbor in the process of deliberately injuring a child, what would be the Christian response? Doing the work of God might very well be to forcefully interfere and protect the child even at the risk of one's own life. Jesus' teaching, "No one has greater love than this, to lay down one's life for one's friends" (Jn. 15:13), would seem to apply. I point this out only to bring into perspective the complexity of human interaction where black and white rules sometimes just don't carry out the work of God.

God's Strategy - Overcome Evil with Good. As I think about it, the Apostle Paul suggests that the Christian response is not to respond to evil with evil, but to overcome evil with good. Does that work? He writes:

> Live in harmony with one another; do not be haughty, but associate with the lowly; do not claim to be wiser than you are. Do not repay anyone evil for evil, but take thought for what is noble in the sight of all. If it is possible, so far as it depends on you, live peaceably with all. Beloved, never avenge yourselves, but leave room for the wrath of God; for it is written, "Vengeance is Mine, I will repay, says the Lord." No, "if your enemies are hungry, feed them; if they are thirsty, give them something to drink; for by doing this you will heap burning coals on their heads." Do not be overcome by evil, but overcome evil with good. (Romans 12:16-21)

This thought of overcoming evil with good is a difficult strategy. The Christian approach is to treat every person with kindness and love. Is doing good to one's enemies for the purpose of dissolving their ill will the only Christian response to their evil actions? The added effect of heaping burning coals on the enemy's head isn't intended to "punish with kindness" but to either win them over as friends or cause them to feel the pain of bad behavior and perhaps change. The added benefit is that acting kindly creates a good spirit in the one acting. I know from experience.

There is a person I am forced to have contact with even though he is unpleasant and difficult to deal with. I recently had a conversation with my wife who finds it equally unpleasant to work with him. I related an incident in which I had done a small kindness for the person. His response was a curt "Thanks," after which he immediately closed the door in my face. I commented to my wife that I treat him with kindness, not because he deserves it. I do it because I don't want to carry the burden of treating him unkindly. The work of God? Yes, if loving mercy is the work of God. In the process I practice my love for God.

Man's Work as God's Work. Another dimension to this question as to what is the work of God emerges where Paul deals with how slaves should behave toward their masters. He writes:

> Slaves, obey your earthly masters in everything; and do it, not only when their eye is on you and to win their favor, but with sincerity of heart and reverence for the Lord. Whatever you do, work at it with all your heart, as working for the Lord, not for men, since you know that you will receive an inheritance from the Lord as a reward. It is the Lord Christ you are serving. (Col. 3:22-24)

Is Paul here condoning slavery? That is hardly imaginable. He is accepting the social order in which he lives, an order that our twenty-first century world almost universally condemns. He finds no moral problem with this order, or he certainly would have stated his view, especially to Philemon. He approaches it from a personal behavior point of view. Masters are to be kind to their slaves, and slaves are not to be rebellious. The escaped slave, Onesimous, is instructed to return to his master, and Philemon the master is instructed not to punish him. Paul simply doesn't address the question of whether slavery is wrong. Slaves are to obey with sincerity and reverence for the Lord.

What Paul does in this passage in Colossians is to give a dignity and worth to all human enterprise. It should be for those in positions of power a reminder that their work is no more the work of God than the work of those with little power and perhaps working for slave wages. It should be to every person who toils a reminder that any toiling that benefits humankind honors God. It should be for the person who will not work a warning that with or without a job, God can be served in any good deed done for another.

This passage of Scripture beautifully affirms that one of the most unmistakable ways in which we love God is in doing our work, whatever it is, as working for God. Notable is the use of the expression "with all your heart." Put your heart into it, we say when a person is discouraged, or just being dilatory in their work. What a waste when the marvelous machinery of the human body with which God has endowed humans is grudgingly employed. What an insult to the great Designer. We may have been designed for greater things than that in which we are employed, but there is, "nothing better for them than to be happy and enjoy themselves as long as they live; moreover, it is God's gift that all should eat and drink and take pleasure in all their toil" (Eccl. 3:12,13).

This concept of doing things "as working for the Lord," applies to all areas of life. Our relationships with our spouses, children, grandchildren, and fellow workers are all a part of, "as working for the Lord." Indeed, this principle may be one of the most visible ways in which we love God. The difference comes in seeing the activity of every moment in the light of living that moment for God. Now, that's loving God! It casts every moment—even the impossible ones—in a new dimension.

Being the Presence of God. The highest of God's work for me is trying to be a Godly presence wherever I am. My puck-guarding friend said he tries to show "love for Him above all else, hourly, daily." I've never been sorry when in a moment of impatience I've done what I think to be the Godly thing. In other moments, when I've not thought about what is the Godly thing I often look back with regret at not finding a better way. Perhaps a practical definition of God's work is, "doing what is the Godly thing in any given moment." His work is to be the embodiment of the presence of God as far as I am able.

Doing God's work more generally, however, must be seen in the light of purpose and action guided by that love. My own purpose statement is, "To love God to my fullest and to be the presence of God in the world." My goals are to be an effective communicator of the gospel, to bring unity among all Godly people, and to help all people reach their full potential.

The work of God has many dimensions. God's work for me at this moment is exploring what it means to love God. I look at the day ahead of me, and what I will be doing. My wife has asked me to take care of a number of things today. Doing those things will show both my love for her and, in a sense, my love for God, as a part of His work for me is being a loving husband.

One of the things I'm exploring is the reality that we become like what we love, which is why loving God is such a powerful force in our lives. I once knew a farmer who loved owning land. The man was defined by his farms. They were important to him above all else, what he thought about almost constantly. Acquiring more land was his singular goal and what he had spent his life pursuing.

He was personified by land as no other person I've ever known. His relationships were for the most part defined by his farms. When he talked with people, he thought about how those people might affect his farm. Would the person he was talking to try to find out what farms he was interested in so they could get there first? Or could the person give him a line on another farm that might be available? I know of very few people he enjoyed just for who they were. I'm sure there were some things he enjoyed—like the nice cars he drove, the home he lived in, the fine livestock he raised and the latest tractors and combines. Even all of these were for him primarily about demonstrating his standing in the farming community.

Yet, he was a Christian man—not a contradiction. Loving more land is no greater sin than hatred, lust, gluttony, slothfulness, gossip, or—name your favorite sin. I could love this man because God loved him, not his farms, and I didn't love his farms. He helped the Church where I was a student minister, sometimes in extravagant ways. Maybe I could say, in fact I will say, I think he loved the church...not merely **his** Church, but the whole church. That may have been his saving grace and the one thing that kept him from becoming a totally self-centered man who didn't care about God.

Bringing Light - Being the Light. In many ways I am my work. For over 30 years I have labored in God's vineyard, tending the vines which produce the fruit for which God's children should be known (by their fruits you shall know them). I cannot say why I chose to be a minister. I believe it chose me. I believe God called me to be a minister.

At the same time I do not believe that I do the work of God any more than a woman in our Church who looks after people who are dealing with problems. She doesn't get paid to do this. No one asked her to take on this role. She gets very little public recognition. I know about her work because those to whom she ministers tell me. Her work is every bit as much the work of God as what I do as a minister.

As I think about it, we are both doing the work of God, but in different roles. The caring woman is more the hands while I am more the head—or maybe the mouth! We both do what we do because we have hearts for God. I love giving the cup of cold water to the thirsty. I gain even greater satisfaction in motivating others to give the cup of water to the thirsty people around them.

In that sense I am a "professional minister." I say that with some hesitation because it could imply something unintended and mercenary. As a professional I devoted over a decade to college and seminary training. I wanted to become a minister who had a deep and examined understanding of God and the Church. I wanted to know my work as thoroughly as a medical doctor or a lawyer or a professor. I wanted to be prepared to do a work worthy of my God.

I wanted to prepare myself to talk with anybody—devout Christian or atheist—and to understand them, while at the same time being understood as a person who knew God. I wanted not only to be a person of faith, but one who could "give a reason for the faith" that is within me. While I wanted to be respected among thinking people for my knowledge of God and Christianity, I also was determined to reflect a broad understanding of the human situation.

Ten years of college and seminary was a long, difficult and sometimes painful journey. For me it was vital to my search for the meaning of God's love and His caring for the universe. In some forty years of ministry I'm still exploring what it means for me, and for humankind, to love God in return, and to do that with all our hearts. I want to love God that much, and as illusive as it is to put that into words, it has been very clear what it demands in action in those times when someone was in need. Sometimes the need was for food. Sometimes the need was for giving insights into how God's love works.

Jesus said that when we give a cup of water to a thirsty person it's as though we give it to Him. He didn't say it, but it's embedded in His teaching, "When you give light to a person living in darkness, you have saved me when I was lost." The work to which I have devoted myself has been the work of being the light in a world that is lost. There is no higher calling, no greater need in this world.

I do not speak of simply making Christians of everyone. My goal is to convey the love of God in Christ to all, in what I teach and in how I live. The mission statement of the Church which I've served most of my life is, "We exist to be the presence of Christ." For me that has meant to carry on the ministry which Christ established. Paul called the Church the "body of Christ." The work of the Church, and my work, is to bring the healing of God to the whole world—physical healing and spiritual healing. When we live that way, devoting our lives to doing what we believe to be God's work, we are loving God with all our hearts.

VI.
Seeing Life Through the Eyes of God

Too Grand to Imagine—Enlarging Our Spirits. The first time I saw the Grand Canyon I was overwhelmed by its vastness. Looking at it was like having my eyeballs expand outside my head in order to take it all in. It just didn't seem possible that something as vast as the Canyon could actually exist. I saw across it, looked down into its depths, gazed at its side canyons and even the river deep within its plunging walls, and reached out with my eyes for its length. The truth is that it was just too vast for me to totally take in and experience.

I have noticed something about the Grand Canyon that always fascinates me. I have this mental image of what it looks like—its color, its shape and even its dimensions. Yet, every time I've walked to the edge of the Canyon—every time!—I am surprised by its vastness. My imagination simply cannot contain its full dimensions.

I have hiked down into the Canyon, explored some of its caves, rafted on its river, and camped in its depths many times. For all that, I encounter it only in very small, incomplete, and fragmented human-scale parts. Maybe that's also the best I can hope for where God is concerned. As Paul writes, "Eye has not seen, nor ear heard, the things God has prepared for those who love Him" (1 Cor. 2:9).

I do have this mental impression of God—not the white-haired bearded man. In fact, it isn't an image at all. Neither is it a Star Trek representation of some force field, some spinning, churning, undulating, ghostly essence. It's more like an all-sensory experience. When I reach out for God in my inner self, when I pray, when I contemplate God, there is no image that I see. It's more a coming together of all my senses, focusing my whole being on experiencing God, the essence of His Spirit.

Trying to experience God isn't greatly different from when I try to get in touch with my self. Eyes closed, sound ignored, touch and taste and smell ignored, the inward eye senses a place at the center that defies description. Try it sometime. Just close your eyes and shut out as best you can all the surrounding sounds and sensations and focus on the inward self. It can, depending on your state of mind, be fascinating. Trying to experience God is, for me, not only different in quality but also in direction. In experiencing self my spirit turns inward. In trying to experience God my spirit reaches outward beyond my self. It is nevertheless an interior experience limited by my awareness.

All of Me Is Not Big Enough to Imagine All of God. I don't think I can really comprehend, let alone experience the full reality of God. I am too limited. We all are. Writers of science fiction have wrestled with some of the issues of the limitations of humans when it comes to experiencing beings of vastly superior ability. In most instances these stories conclude that if the beings are sufficiently superior to humans, they choose to remain hidden, waiting for humans to develop the capability of communicating and interacting on a higher plane.

One writer wrote of a fictional being that was in the form of a cloud passing through our galaxy. The being communicated instructions on the construction of an apparatus which, when placed on a man's head, would allow him to receive the knowledge of the being. Upon wearing the apparatus and initiating contact the man's brain was destroyed in the attempt to transfer the knowledge imparted by the being. So much for exceeding our limits!

Yet we are driven to exceed our limits. It's a part of our nature. In the Olympics the goal is not only to win but also to set new records, to go beyond what anyone has done before. Why should it be any different in the spiritual dimension? I don't feel driven to go beyond where anyone else has gone spiritually. I do wish to go as far as I am capable of going and to continue the attempt to expand that limit.

A Growing, Changing, Dynamic Process. A woman I have known for over thirty years told me that loving God for her is a growing, changing, dynamic process. As she grows, her love grows. As she changes, her love for God changes to parallel what she is becoming. This woman has served God diligently during all the years I've known her. Her efforts to teach and to help others have continued through the years. Yet she says her love for God is a changing, developing process.

Does that mean she didn't really love God fully at any time in the past? Or does it mean that the same love has expanded to greater and greater dimensions? As our experiences in serving God expand, and as our knowledge of God expands, so our capacity for love expands. This book is an effort to expand my own capacity for love, and to motivate others to expand their capacity to love God.

It is the full dimensions of God for which I continue to search—to know God. The search expands my consciousness of the earth and the universe. In this existence I know that I can never see God. My spiritual eyes are not yet big enough, wonderful enough or possessed of sensors enough to see God. I think my soul can catch just a glimmer of God. I try imagining God in the hope I'll be able to see and experience a bit of God within. I can't claim to even have come close, but I fancy that perhaps I have made progress.

On our honeymoon my wife and I explored around Lake Superior. Semiprecious gemstones called agates are found in that area, and they are very pretty and fascinating creations. We spent a few hours searching for them. We knew what they looked like from having seen one that I had found some years before. As we looked we knew they were there and in our minds we created images of finding them. When one appeared it was not unexpected. It was the fulfillment of something we had already visualized within.

I can imagine experiencing, or sensing God within myself. In fact there have been times when I would claim, if only to myself, that I have experienced a small infinitesimal atom of the essence of God. I can't create it at will. I can't cause others to experience it, though I have tried. But just as when I've searched for agates I could imagine coming upon one, so I can imagine stumbling upon that place within where, at last, I actually see that part of myself that I believe exists within—the image of God. I know that's a search for a mystical experience, but isn't that what any search for God is? It's certainly more than a mere intellectual experience.

I think it happens occasionally, in fleeting moments that pass too quickly for me to capture. Sometimes when the "me" is suppressed to the place where I gaze beyond myself, at least in my imagination, I make a connection with "being" which seems always to be there just below the surface of my awareness. It's an interesting experience, perhaps described by an ancient who declares that God has, "put a sense of past and future into their minds, yet they cannot find out what God has done from the beginning to the end" (Eccl. 3:11). Maybe we can't discover ALL of what God has done, but I want to discover as much as is humanly possible.

Becoming Like our God. James Harriet, an English veterinarian and gifted storyteller, relates some of his remarkable experiences in caring for ailing animals. He delightfully spins the tale of one elderly couple that occasionally calls on him to care for their little dog. Harriet notes that the particular breed of dog owned by this couple is ordinarily affectionate and sweet tempered. This particular pet, however, is the opposite. It responds aggressively and belligerently to the vet's attempts to examine and diagnose its condition. Harriet finds this unusual and chalks it off to the poor luck of this couple in acquiring the odd one that was unfortunately not representative of the breed.

The old dog finally dies and the couple is distraught. Some time later they call Harriet and he is delighted to hear they have replaced their pet with another of the same breed. Happily he finds this one to have the pleasant characteristics for which its kind is noted. A couple of years later he is called back to the home when the dog develops some malady. To his immense surprise he discovers that the dog has acquired the same mean disposition that he had found in its predecessor.

He was at a loss to explain what it was in the household that resulted in two such unlikely ill-tempered dogs. Was it simply bad luck, or were they responding to unseen influences in the home? The man and woman were to all appearances kindly and caring, but it caused him to wonder. The implication was that each little animal had acquired a disposition that reflected something not readily apparent in the owners.

Though there are notable exceptions, it's generally recognized that children often grow up exhibiting many of the same characteristics seen in their parents. My brother and I have had some enjoyable talks about what characteristics of mom and dad we recognize in ourselves. We just can't help ourselves. We see life through their eyes. Kind and loving parents are likely to have children who are kind and loving. "The acorn doesn't fall far from the tree," is one way we express this or, "Like father like son."

Is it also, "Like Father God like God's children?" It seems likely that a person's understanding and experience of God shape that person's characteristics and behaviors. A person who sees God as loving and forgiving probably is a loving and forgiving person. A person who understands God as judgmental and harsh most likely will reflect that same judgmental nature. That's a great reason to search for the deepest understanding of God's love as possible.

The Purpose of Man –The Incarnation of God? We say we worship God. What if God also in a sense "worships" us?—Well, not really **worships**. Doting parents come to mind. We praise God for the wonder of His gift and The Gift. Do we not also feel the praise of God when we do well? Is not worship a mutual praise between two beings as much as abject bowing of subject to master—the inferior to the superior? Oh, of course we are not equals in powers or knowledge or wisdom, but equals in love. Is it possible that God created us so that He could experience love?

Where was love before the creation of the world? If God existed always, what did God love before He created the world? Did He merely dash from galaxy to galaxy absorbing the wonders of the universe, exalting in the great volcano of Mars, basking in the glow of the Orion Nebula, playing with black holes and quasars? Did God amuse himself by nudging a few asteroids together and creating a planet? Did He "breathe" on a cold surface leaving behind condensed water and assorted gases from His breath and maybe a tree or two? What would God do all day in a lifeless wonderland? And what would He love?

So was there anything for God to love before humankind? Oh yes, I suppose one could say that animals can love, but I don't know what that would mean for a brachiopod or even a dinosaur. A new level of love became possible with the creation of humans. It is humankind's emerging love—for others and ultimately for God—that God could not create and could not experience alone. Humans had to develop the capacity for love within themselves out of their own awareness and experience. Some religions explain this as the developing awareness by humankind that a Creator had breathed into humans the breath of life. As humankind developed the idea of loving God the capacity to love God emerged and a loving relationship developed.

It is never said in Scripture that one is to love parents with all their heart, soul, mind and strength. That highest level of love is to be reserved for God alone. This is crucial to our quest to understand what that level of love demands and confers. God as "Father" opens the door to a new understanding of God. It also demolishes our attempts to restrict our love of God to only the dimension of a human father. This is one of Jesus' singular contributions to our understanding of love that exists between God and His children. Ah, but to understand the full dimensions of that love—that is our quest. As Paul writes to the Romans,

> Oh, the depth of the riches of the wisdom and knowledge of God! How unsearchable His judgments, and His paths beyond tracing out! "Who has known the mind of the Lord? Or who has been His counselor?" (Rom. 11:33, 34)

The Redeemed Life. My grandmother Hostetler probably truly loved God more than anything else. There seemed to be around her the very essence of the Spirit of God. Her life was defined by prayer and meditation, by doing good—especially for her twelve children and dozens of grandchildren. Her kindnesses to many children in our town flowed from a Godly and loving heart. She spoke of God freely and often, acknowledging Him as a constant reality in her life.

She quoted Scripture, but even more, she lived it. She would rise early in the morning for her prayer and devotion time. You couldn't be around her without experiencing the soft, gentle, accepting love of God that was within her. It totally shaped her life and you could see God in her. It came quite naturally to her, dominating her conversation. She connected God with about everything she did. She didn't even think about it. It's just who she was. She witnessed, un-self-consciously and without being obnoxious or invasive of the other person's point of view. It wasn't merely what she said. It was her manner of love. Her Scripture quoting, of which she was hugely adept, was sprinkled into every conversation. It's what she liked to talk about...but it wasn't all she talked about.

I think she took advantage of every opportunity to influence her grandchildren. We sometimes listened beyond what we would have found interesting because she spent time with us. "Just look at how God designed this little plant. Look at that praying mantis kneeling before God. How wonderful that trees point toward heaven. They remind us that we're to keep our eyes on heaven." It was the most natural thing you can imagine. It's who she was and how she lived.

I believe that even she, however, would say along with the Apostle Paul, "Not that I have...already reached the goal, but I press on to make it my own" (Phil. 3:12). We live somewhere between what we were before we committed our lives to Christ and where we hope to be as totally redeemed persons.

The people who I have seen as being the closest to God were in some ways ordinary people who yet were spectacular in their love for God and life. They lived, as far as I could tell, redeemed lives. They lived in a state of love.

This leads me to conclude that the Promised Land of loving God with ALL my heart, the ultimate goal, is not out there in some future moment in time. It's right here where I stand. Recognizing that... accepting that...rejoicing in that—**that** is loving God in a moment of crescendo. I think God is honored and feels loved when I say, "I love this very moment, and it's the best that this moment can be for me." If in another moment I get swept up in a detour of selfishness, that's human and, I ask God to forgive me. At the same time I know He continues to call me back to complete love.

When I attend a symphony concert and it's boring or poorly done I sit waiting for it to end. When the program is interesting and well-done I enjoy each movement for what it is. I do not wait for, or even yearn for, the conclusion of the symphony. I can simply say that I do not need the finish of any symphony to fully enjoy its continuum. A "reprise," if there is one, is recognition that even when the symphony concludes, it isn't finished. It isn't about the conclusion. It's about the rise and fall of every phrase. This is to say that at this moment I feel I have finished, I have redeemed, and I have enjoyed life, if not to its fullest, at least to the fullest of what is possible for me at this moment.

That provides the impetus to take the next step with the expectation that every step is its own finish. It does not have to be better than the last, or more grand and lofty. It merely needs to be the next and to be appreciated for all its possibilities, for all its redeemed potential. Loving God gives me confidence that love's highest achievement is worth attempting and its most disappointing failure endurable and meaningful.

We are God's Canvas. To love God is to cherish in our heart all He has done, and to provide the canvas upon which He continues to paint. Is it possible that we are the living canvas upon which God paints? How would God paint a masterpiece, even for His own pleasure? No canvas smaller than the universe would be adequate. No composition that did not include humankind could express His imagination. Even then, humans are quite limited and limiting for our eyes have not yet seen, nor our ears heard the things that God has prepared for those who love Him (see: 1 Cor. 2:9). Limiting or not, so far as we know we're the best that God has created. I do not say that with egotistical pride. In fact, I can imagine that we, in partnership with God, are creating something even higher—a more complete medium upon which God and we can compose together. How so?

Without man would God ever have heard the music of an orchestra, or a violin? Of course, there are the songs of birds and whales and such but, arguably, they are lacking in the complexity and variety of human composers. Could God compose music more fulfilling, more engaging, than Beethoven? If He did, who would play it? Who is the judge of what the best music would be? If God alone were judge, what appeals to Him might sound as cacophony to humans. Is it possible that God is looking for someone to, not only compose and play the symphony of the universe, but someone to go with Him to the performance?

It was my incredible and unlikely honor to be allowed to enter the Kivas of the Hopi Indians back in the 90's. Outsiders are no longer permitted to enter these sacred places. Through the influence of a man who was known as the "White Navajo," a youth group I was leading was invited to attend the Bean Dance. No pictures were allowed, but the beauty of the elaborately costumed mudheads and kachinas is painted on my mind. Their music also—flutes and drums mostly, I remember, and there were probably other instruments, the names of which I would not recognize. The haunting melody and rhythms of their musicians and the movements of the dancers was a ballet of exquisite beauty. How could it be improved upon?

It was its own fullness, a complete development of that dance and music. To add one violin would have made it something different, destroying the original. I would not want to imagine this world without that singular music. I believe God enjoys it too, and that He listens from His permanent place in the theatre of this world, not in a premiere box seat, not as the conductor, but as the most appreciative opera buff sitting front row center. Perhaps, I imagine, He is occasionally tempted to leap onto the stage and take up an instrument to save a faltering passage. But He has limited Himself to merely providing encouragement and direction for those who would be His musicians.

God's Eyes. Among some groups of Indians in both the Western United States and northwestern Mexico there is a devotional weaving known as an *Ojo de Dios*, or Eye of God. For these people the weaving represents the many facets of our world that are mysteries—things beyond our understanding. It acknowledges that there are realities which we cannot see, yet artfully captures the mystery of existence which exists but cannot be explained.

It has occurred to me that our very desire to know and understand God, while a mystery, is itself a step toward seeing God. Oh, I don't mean actually looking on God as one would look upon a tree or a mountain, as though God could be compressed into such a limited form. Humans have constructed idols from ancient times, and limited though those idols may be they represent the human desire to see the image deep within themselves—the image of God.

The Bible, of course, forbids the construction of such physical representations of God; however, the Bible also affirms that man is made in the image of God. So in a way, looking upon another human being is to look upon a representation, a visible form, of God. It makes me uncomfortable to express it that way. It seems too familiar to compare God to a human, but the idea is found in the Bible. Jesus said, "Whoever has seen Me has seen the Father" (John 14:9). If humans are created in the image of God then, in a sense, God is seen in every human. Some seem grotesquely malformed, yet even in the most evil of humans there exists perhaps, a distorted reflection of God's image.

As I contemplate this mysterious connection between God and man I can't help but wonder if God, Who is a spirit, in a sense sees the world through our eyes? How can a spirit see? What is a spirit's perspective? Why did God become a man? We believe He did it in order to fully relate to us and to allow us to fully relate to Him. Jesus was "in the form of God...but emptied Himself... being born in human likeness" (Phil 2:5-8).

In Jesus, mankind experienced God. At the same time, God experienced humanness—all of humanness. In Jesus we understand the reality that God sees the world through our eyes. We also become the eyes of God, which is why it's so important for us to look only upon that which is worthy of God. That's the "responsibility" side.

The "wonder" side is that seeing, experiencing, thinking, pondering, creating—all those things that are so wondrously human, can be understood as the Spirit God experiencing the world in all its splendor. We will, in this life, never come closer to seeing God than in seeing, not only each other, but all of life. Life is the presence of God.

Wow! Doesn't that open a whole new dimension of understanding the world and the universe? Doesn't that explain why we humans keep expanding our search of the universe as well as the tiniest little fragment of matter? It is God Who is exploring and experiencing the universe through our eyes. Yes, we are God's canvas, but how marvelous to come to the realization that the canvas is gazing back at us and in its eyes we see God.

Through the Eyes of Turtles and Geese. As I muse on this I am sitting on a balcony overlooking a beautiful lake in Southern

Illinois. I notice a small commotion in the water at the lake's edge. The activity merges into a small group of turtles that crawl out of the water onto a slab of rock a few feet off shore. It's a cold but very sunny day and shortly the little band of turtles is soaking up the afternoon sun, a brief escape from the unrelenting cold of the deep lake.

If God sees the world through my eyes, which I think is likely, does He not also see the world through the turtles' eyes? Yes, I'm sure it's true that God glides through the water in the form of those turtles experiencing the exhilaration of living the unique, though admittedly limited, experience of an aquatic being. I'm fully aware of how naive this view is—at first. It's also a profound understanding of life and its connection with God.

After some time the turtles one by one slipped back into the water and were gone. Only a few minutes later a small gaggle of geese flew over my little bay, turned, and floated down out of the air and landed noisily near the same rock the turtles had occupied only moments before. They began foraging around the shoreline, enjoying a feast of whatever it is that geese make such a fuss about.

Shortly one of them climbed up on the same rock previously occupied by the turtles, enjoying a little leisure in the warm sunshine. I found myself looking at the lake and the sky through the eyes of that goose. Yes, I really could rather vividly imagine what it was experiencing. Is God capable of less? If I were God would I not long for the joy of gliding through clear water, and floating along on the currents of the air? Could I want for a better flying form than that of a goose?

The geese have gone now, flown away to some other water more blue on the other side of the lake. They didn't finish the full potential of what was in this little moment of shoreline, at least I can't imagine that they did, but apparently what they gathered was sufficient for now. I am certain that another wandering gaggle could arrive and find something more, and different. Every moment is sufficient—and different.

What a contrast! Turtles and geese—and a human observing from a distance—all were experiencing the same little piece of earth and lake. How wonderful to see through my own inward eye the aerial approach as a goose, to glide to a landing, to float upon the water and bask in the sun on the dry rock...to take to my wings and fly high above. I compared what I had seen through the eyes of the turtles with what I had seen through the eyes of the geese. God is in all things. He truly sees through the eyes of the turtles, the geese, and us humans.

Through the Eyes of God. I desire to love God in order to see, understand, experience and celebrate the wealth of my own life. When I was young I think I failed to appreciate the riches of the ordinary, the wealth of the wilderness, the selflessness of exalting in and embracing of even my own limitations.

I am spending my life attempting to understand our universe through the eyes of God. I hypothesize God as a plausibility, not as a retreat or superstition, but as the most likely explanation of the presence of life in the universe. All around me I see a multi-faceted wonder of plants and animals in unimaginable variety. How incredible, miraculous even, if all that were purely the result of chance and natural selection. That would require great faith in chance. God is easier to believe in.

The existence of the physical universe is explainable without hypothesizing an Arranging or Creating, or Acting, One. What process caused the emergence of an orderly arrangement of energy is what both science and theology attempt to explain. An explanation of the origin of that energy is not required in order to understand its nature, behavior, and essence. Both science and religion find it important to attempt to reach a plausible explanation. The scientific explanation that it just happened is a pretty fine "retreat" in itself, and one undeniably based on ignorance by definition. Of course it's possible that science will one day remove that ignorance, but it doesn't seem likely.

In the meantime the God Who created it is content with experiencing it through the eyes and ears He put in His creatures, including you and me.

VII.
Loving Means Listening

The Silent God. I would not say it's impossible to love someone without talking to them. We love babies who can't talk back to us in words, but that's different because they respond in other ways. One of the first signs that love is breaking down between people, whether a husband and wife, parents and children or two friends, is that they cease talking to each other.

How can we love God if we don't talk to Him? How can God claim to love us if He doesn't talk back when we talk to him? I don't mean that to be trite, in fact, the opposite. In the difficult times of our lives when we desperately need a word from God we would love to hear His voice. Yes, we have what we know to be His words in the Bible, but they are words to humankind in general. Of course we pray to Him, but that's us talking to Him, and most people I know do not hear Him talking back in an audible voice.

Even the Psalmist is vexed by this silence of God.

> Answer me when I call, O God of my right! You gave me room when I was in distress. Be gracious to me, and hear my prayer.... But know that the LORD has set apart the faithful for Himself; the LORD hears when I call to Him. (Ps. 4:1, 3)

Again he writes,

> You have seen, O LORD; do not be silent! O Lord, do not be far from me! Wake up! Bestir Yourself for my defense, for my cause, my God and my Lord! Vindicate me, O LORD, my God, according to Your righteousness, and do not let them rejoice over me. (Ps. 35:22-23)

Understanding this silence of God is essential to understanding what it means to love God. Make no mistake. It does not come naturally, this listening for God. Even people of faith often do not understand. It requires listening in ways different from listening for men. Listening for God requires the rock-solid confidence that He hears. We hear no reassuring voice saying, "Uh huh. Yes, go on my child, go on, I hear you." Our usual understanding of communication is challenged.

What If You Got What You Asked For? Here's where we often get it wrong and expect a human response from God. Yes, we long for His audible voice, "Samuel, Samuel," even beg for it just so we can satisfy our human senses. If it were given, if we really heard, would that solve it once and for all? Hardly. Our next request would surely be, "Are You STILL there?" If God responded to that test with a reassuring, "Yes, I'm still here," it is likely that our next request would be something like, "I'm hungry. I pray that You turn that stone into bread." Suppose it happened? Impressed with our success, it would be only human to keep asking for more—a nicer car, a bigger house, a better job, bending other people to our needs and desires.

Assured now of our own power to bend God to our desires, would we not then be tempted to ask Him for invincibility? By now we would have noticed that all other believers had been similarly elevated in success. To keep our edge we would require that we be free from harm, either from them or ourselves. Our prayer might be, "Save me from even my own deliberately dangerous acts." Note that this progression follows the order of the temptations of Jesus (Lk. 4:1-14).

God will have none of that. It goes all the way back to the Psalmist's request, and ours; "Do not be silent…! Bestir yourself for my defense…. Vindicate me" (Ps. 35:22-24). It just doesn't work that way. If it did, there would be as many gods as there are people. No one would be satisfied until he was at the top of the heap. No one would stop asking until she was God.

Think about it. If God were to respond as the all-powerful genie in the bottle, there would be little reason for us to take care of ourselves. Why would we? All we would have to do would be to ask… and there would be no end to the asking.

The childhood story of the fisherman and the flounder cleverly speaks to this point. The fisherman catches the mythical talking fish that promises him that if he tosses him back he'll grant any wish. The fisherman recognizes a good deal when he hears one. He asks for a nice house and tosses the fish back. Returning home he finds his little hut is gone and his wife is in a nice cottage. He remarks to her that now they will be happy, to which she responds, "We'll see." You guessed it, the wife sends him back to the fish again…and again…and again, each time asking for more, finally asking to be able to control the rising and setting of the sun. "Go back," the fish responds. "You'll find your wife in the hut where you started."

We ask God to speak to us, then to defend us and finally to favor us above all others. His whispered response is, "Go back. I'm with you, and that will have to be enough. No voice, no suspending of the laws of physics and no special favors. I've already given you all that you need to succeed. My favor rests upon those who do My will."

The Inner Whisper. Our prayer then becomes in itself an act of faith. "God, I know You're there, and I'm going to act on that confident awareness." In prayer we acknowledge what God has already done—far beyond what we have asked, and what He continues to do even without our asking. In prayer we hear the inner voice as it says:

Step into the water. If it doesn't part, ask for My strength and swim across.
Wandering in the wilderness? Ask for My guidance and I'll lead you through.
Hungry? Pray and observe how I care for the birds and the flowers.
Are you sick or in distress? Pray for My peace and expect My courage.

We talk to God on His terms, not ours. The basic premise of prayer is that we approach God with our thanks and requests and He determines the response. The most likely response comes to us, not in a voice out of the night, but the inner whisper of His Spirit, and sometimes the voice of another person.

Jesus makes a startling observation about how God speaks when He encounters a crowd of worshipers in Jerusalem. Some Pharisees demand of Him, "Teacher, order Your disciples to stop." Jesus answers, "If these were silent, the stones would shout out" (Lk. 19:39, 40).

I understand this to mean, "You're hearing the voice of God in those people, but your ears are closed." God does not speak to us out of thin air. Sometimes people speak to us instead of stones and their words carry the voice of God. It's the way God is heard. Get used to it. Count on it. Listen for it. He gave us ears to hear, but often we don't listen, or listen in the wrong way. We should pray for discerning ears.

In the garden Jesus prays for—pleads for—the intervention of God: "If it is possible, let this awful suffering be averted." Within Himself He hears the voice of God telling him to accept the reality that the suffering is necessary and to proceed with carrying out the will of God. A booming voice would not be more convincing. There is no voice out of the night. There is the inner assurance that He is on the intended and necessary path (Matt. 26:36-46).

How strange that at Jesus' baptism there is the voice out of heaven, "This is my Son...," but in another far greater test on the cross there is only silence. Strange? Not really. Baptism is itself, the voice of God if we have ears to hear. The waters speak and promise, "buried, yet you shall be raised with Christ" (Rom. 6:4). On the cross so silent is God that Jesus cries out asking why God has forsaken Him. God answers in Jesus' own words from the cross, "It is finished" (Jn. 19:30). How could Jesus have said those triumphant words unless they had been given by God?

The skeptic will not accept this. Their very disbelief makes them deaf to the voice of God. He would speak to them also, but they refuse to listen, or are distracted by the cares of life. They will hear only on their own terms. Yet God continues to speak to all His children—all creatures, really. If we listen we can almost hear:

It's time to fly south for the winter. Come, let's fly. I'll enjoy the journey with you.

You've been at sea long enough. Follow Me to your birth-stream in Alaska.

Leave Ur, and follow Me to a place I'll show you. You'll know when you're there.

Don't give in to the cancer. Give in to Me. I'm stronger.

Don't be afraid. Do what you already know I've asked of you.

What part of "I love you" do you not understand? Love you? You're My child!

One who listens for God does not need to have the ear drums vibrate. Her spirit resonates with God's Spirit and she hears. Call it an inner voice, call it a vision, or call it a whisper. It's the way God speaks. His children know His voice (Jn. 10:3-5).

Guidance from Beyond Myself. Probably every praying person has experienced moments in which they feel they have been given direction from God. Whether such direction has a reality in actual communication from God or is the result of insights the praying person has in the process of meditation cannot be demonstrated scientifically. Even the believer doesn't always know for certain. Each person must determine for himself if the direction came from his own reason, or in some way from God.

In my own experience I must say there have been many occasions in which I was convinced—yes, really certain, that valuable direction came to me through prayer. Whether it was the power of my own reasoning or superimposed wisdom from the voice of God within, it felt like guidance from beyond myself. I know it wasn't me. This is one of the ways in which God is real to me. Every time I've felt that a thought came from God, it has turned out to be not only right, but important and crucial to turning points—or continuing points—in my life.

That doesn't mean that every important decision I've made was done in consultation with God. There have been plenty of times when my thoughts were, "God expects me to figure this one out on my own." Sometimes those occasions have turned out well, and sometimes not. I made such decisions with the understanding that no matter the outcome, I would accept the results.

Let me explain how prayer has been valuable at the crucial times. In none of these important events have I felt the laws of the universe were interfered with on my behalf, or on behalf of those for whom I've prayed. There haven't been any such events that I am aware of. The benefit was in arriving at a decision that seemed beyond my ability or reason. Some of these decisions were unlikely, some seemingly illogical, and some were just plain surprising to me.

I acknowledge that the feeling of certainty I have in God's involvement in these events may involve a bit of reading back into them the benefit derived from prayer. I try to be as objective as possible in determining if the outcome was indeed a good, or the right, outcome. But then, how can I be sure if any result is good or bad—or the degree to which it might be the best or worst? Who knows? A different path might have been better, or at least no worse. Loving and trusting God causes me to accept whatever the outcome as the best outcome.

God Told Me. One Sunday morning as I was visiting our Sunday School classrooms greeting our teachers, a young woman approached me. She informed me, "God told me this morning that He wants me to teach the Junior High class." Ordinarily I would have thanked God for the gift and quickly accepted the offer. This time I wasn't so eager. I had talked with this woman before and was not comfortable with her beliefs. I didn't doubt that she loved God, the first test, but

I doubted her suitability for teaching impressionable young students. In short, there was no way I was going to let her teach any class. But what was I to say? "God had told her."

I talked with her for a minute, trying to think of a graceful and kind way to refuse her offer. I listen for some answer from God in moments of uncertainty, but the answer is seldom instantaneous. She was adamant. The voice of God had been real to her. I really do trust God to guide me in such situations and as I talked to her the response came to me. "How strange that God told you He wanted you to teach the Jr. High class," I said to her. "He's telling me that He doesn't want you to teach that class."

I had not heard the voice of God audibly—and I wasn't lying. The inner voice which I perceive to be the Spirit of God within was saying, "It's not a good thing for her to be put in a position to guide young people." I felt that whatever voice she had heard was no more valid than the inner voice I was hearing. The subsequent course of her life validated my belief. My view is that if God really had told her to teach the class He would have directed me to let her.

God Provides. On another occasion I invoked a variation of that approach in a difficult phone conversation. A woman called and began criticizing me for not having organized a Vacation Bible School for the children of our new Church. "I can't believe our Church doesn't have a Vacation Bible School," she accused. "We are neglecting our children and I'm calling to see what you're going to do about it."

I was the only minister of this new Church—its custodian, adult class teacher, youth minister, evangelist, building developer, and everything else that is required of a founding minister. This woman and her family were very active in the Church, leaders who got things done and highly respected by myself, and others. If we didn't have a VBS, she let me know, it was likely they would look for another Church that did.

I began to search my mind for a way to meet her demands. I prayed silently to God to give me the right words. It doesn't always happen, but the right words have come to me often enough that I have come to rely on words from God when I ask. "I'll tell you the reason we don't have a VBS," I heard myself saying as the words came to me in an instant. "We don't have a VBS because we haven't had a director...until now!" There was a long pause during which I allowed the words and the Spirit to do their work on her. "Okay, I'll do it," she said. She ran the best VBS I could have hoped for, and continued to do so every year until she and her family moved to another state.

Our Fallible Senses. What was the difference between how I looked to God for guidance with this woman and the one who had told me God had told her to teach a class? Frankly, I have trouble knowing what it means when a person says, "God told me." Did they hear an audible voice that I would have heard if present? Did they hear an inner voice so compelling that it could be none other than God? Or did they simply have a feeling or a thought that they described as God telling them?

Making a statement that "God told me," carries such audacity that one should be mighty sure it's God Who is speaking, and not merely one's own perception. In the case of the would-be teacher I was sure that she was mistaken. Further, I had confidence that my own view of the matter was every bit as much God's direction to me as she was claiming. In the case of the VBS director, I can't claim that God gave me the words, but I cannot honestly claim they originated with me. If anything, I would say that God spoke to me through her saying, "What are you waiting for? Start a VBS, and here's the person I've chosen to do it."

I relate these instances for two reasons. First, we must admit that what we attribute to God is based on very fallible senses. I've seen people claiming the direction of God succeeding marvelously, and others claiming equal direction failing miserably. I always take their claims seriously—and always am skeptical. Even when they succeed no one can be certain they had been led by God. The law of averages applies even when mistakenly claiming God's direction.

In my own experience, seeking the guidance of God causes me to apply a different set of values and criteria to a decision. I've definitely felt direction from God in my life and continue to seek His guidance when I'm uncertain of how to proceed. At the same time I'm very aware that when I seek God's guidance in prayer I'm also looking at the situation through what I perceive to be the eyes of God. The question, "What does God want me to do?" changes my perspective. I can remember none of these situations turning out badly when I followed what I perceived to be God's direction. I sense an "Other Reality" when I seek God's guidance.

Yet this "Other" is so closely integrated in my "self" that I can only understand it in terms of God somehow being an integral part of me. There are many Scriptures which state that God and Christ are in us. (Jn. 14:15, 16; I Cor. 3:16, *et al.*) This "Other" within is infallible, but my capacity for interpreting the directions of the "Other" is not infallible. It remains for me a "Reality" that I have come to trust...and to love. In relating what I sense of this "Other's" direction I'm always careful to say, "I *believe* God wants us to take this direction."

Prayers for Life Direction. There have been several crossroads in my life where I can remember agonizing in prayer over a decision that would affect the course of my life. It's been at those junctures that I've most intensely put prayer to the test. When I say, "test," I don't mean that prayer was on a "pass/fail" scale. It was more that I was counting on prayer to provide me with wisdom, and sometimes, courage. I knew prayer would assist me.

I've already related the decision early in my ministry where I had a choice to remain where I was in New Jersey, or go to the far country of Arizona. Throughout the day, before I had promised a decision, I had been consulting God in prayer. In truth, I had been doing this for a week, but in the closing hours of the day there was an intense focus brought on by the looming "hour of decision."

My wife and I had discussed the decision for hours. I know she had been praying about it also. It impacted her at least as much as me—in some ways more. She was carrying our first child, and knew we were making a decision about what was best for it and the other children we hoped to have. The Church in New Jersey was within a gated community, which was unlike the neighborhoods in which we had both grown up. They were wonderful people but the community's life-style was quite different from what either of us knew. She had concerns that this might not be the place for a minister fresh out of seminary to get a sympathetic start.

Her family lived in the east and a move would take her far away from people who were dear to her. A couple of years in Arizona didn't seem unbearable after which, she reasoned, we could move back to familiar territory. She recalls praying for guidance— guidance for both of us, knowing that the decision would impact the rest of our lives. After discussing all of this at length she left the decision to me.

Sometime before midnight I began to pray with earnest pleading—not desperately, but passionately. "God, I've dedicated my life to ministry, so I'm expecting some guidance—not demanding, but asking, and yes, expecting." I'm reading back into my prayer, but those were some of my feelings. "If You wanted me in Arizona surely You could have arranged for a higher salary. Why, dear God, is this being so difficult? Answer me that. Are You putting me on Balaam's ass, which unaccountably sees a danger, not in proceeding, but in stopping where I am? Are You trying to move me on to where there is less certainty but more possibility? I have waited, I've watched, and I've prayed. Please, dear Heavenly Father, give me direction." That was pretty much my prayer.

At some point there was a growing awareness that something was happening in my mind, or perhaps one would say, in my heart and soul. The uncertainty in the decision diminished, very gradually, and a new certainty grew. It was to me a surprising, and even astonishing, reversal of uncertainties. The process of prayer had moved me to discover uncertainty in what had been certain, and certainty— CERTAINTY, in what had been uncertain. I turned off the lights, woke my sleeping wife and said, "Marion, we're going to Arizona." "That's nice," she said.

How prayer works, I will not presume to say. I don't think it changes physical laws. I don't think it operates selectively, healing this person and abandoning that person. I pray for God to do some things, like healing or making it possible for the Church to build a building we need, or to watch over my children, for world peace, for the safe return of a soldier. In those prayers I do not intend to invoke "magic." Whether I say it or not, I always pray with the attitude of Jesus in the garden, after praying that His crucifixion be avoided, "Not My will, but Yours."

Prayers for Healing. I continue to pray for healing for people, not as demands but as letting God know what's in my heart. Sometimes the results have been surprising. Among the most memorable and perhaps the most helpful prayers I've offered was for a man who wasn't happy that I was visiting him. We both found ourselves in one of those uncomfortable, yet unavoidable meetings requested by his mother who was my parishioner. He was dying of AIDS and yet, even *in extremis* he was kind enough not to say "no" to his mother and had agreed to my visit. I never like to intrude my presence where I'm unwelcome, feeling that whatever good I may do is far outweighed by the damage. "Darned preachers (I've cleaned up the language here!) won't even let a man die in peace." I knew also that it would be hurtful to the mother if I didn't go. As it turned out, she knew best.

He looked warily at me as I entered the room, recognizing that this was not a doctor whose visit brought him any hope or comfort. I introduced myself and acknowledged that his mother had insisted I come to visit him, and that I would be brief and as un-intrusive as possible. I extended my hand to shake his, and noticed his slight hesitation, which I recognized as his fear of rejection. As he took my hand I held it gently but firmly and the full length of what seemed natural and a little more to let him know I cared and wasn't afraid to touch him. Even at the moment I realized that my hand, unwaveringly holding his, might be the only prayer offered in that visit—the God in me reaching out and touching a man who felt he was an outcast.

I reassured him that I had not come to "put religion on him" and that most of all I didn't want to cause him more distress. I told him I really did care about his pain and discomfort and that I only wanted to help, if that was possible. He relaxed and said he was glad that I had come. I knew he was a musician so I asked him if the memory of his music continued to bring him joy. He said it did, and then told me about some of the music he'd played, and a little that he'd written. He smiled from time to time, as I'm sure some notes played across the instrument of his mind.

As promised, in a few minutes I told him I would leave, but that I'd return if he asked for me. I then said, "It isn't necessary, but if you'd like, I'll offer a prayer." "That will be okay," he replied. My prayer was brief, thanking God for the pleasure this man's music had brought to others, and asking God to give him music in his heart, and comfort and peace and strength. I acknowledged and affirmed the faith the man had told me he had in God. I held his hand as I prayed, which again I sensed was the best, most meaningful prayer I could give.

As I left I stopped at the foot of his bed and turned to face him. I raised my hand and said, "May God bless you." He looked at me, not unkindly. As I reached the door he called out to me, "Dr. Hostetler." I turned and saw that he'd raised his hand as I had raised mine, and he said, "May God bless you, too." I smiled and nodded and left him to his journey. He did't ask for me to return, and I sensed I'd done all I could for him—and he for me. His blessing is with me still. "May God bless you, too."

I know God better because of prayer. At the same time, prayer has helped me know and love others better as well. In loving others through prayers I can say those prayers have been, for me, a most satisfying expression of loving God.

VIII.
Loving without Seeing

"**I'll Let You Know...I Promise.**" Voice colored with awe, the lovely lady related her experience of a message from beyond this world. It had been some years since her husband of forty-five years had died, but the memories of those days were still beautiful on her face. Before he departed this world from Washington, D.C. he had enjoyed some months of preparation for the journey—more a preparation of his wife for her being left behind than for his unavoidable looming departure.

With little hint of sorrow she told of their precious days together in the lingering sunset of his life, and how they talked of good times and bad as though they were the same. He knew his approaching journey would be easier than her lonely watch, both in the approach, the boarding of that final train, and then the fading into the distance. "Don't worry," he had told her. "I'll let you know of my safe arrival, I promise."

The summer came, but its green trees could not delay the looming autumn. Soon the leaves had fallen and the dogwood tree outside his window mirrored the draining of the life of his failing branches, and he was gone. Sad were those days. Though well prepared, she felt the shortening of her own days as the chill winds of life blew unnoticed through her own stripped branches. There was life, but only in the roots. It did not reach unto the heavens.

Winter came, and soon the white painting of the snow brought some comfort. That which is dark cannot resist the fairy dusting of the crystal cold, somehow coloring over even the deep trenches of sorrow. One day, in early January, the sun shone sparkling on the now blank and unspoiled snow-covered face of mother earth. The dogwood tree that stood outside what had been his window, against all nature, sprouted buds which went unnoticed for a day or two. Then the flowers blossomed forth—life defying the cold of winter, and the lady noticed—and released her sorrow. "I promise."

"If You're Really There"—Why It Matters. "If you're really there God, send a meteor across the night sky. It doesn't have to be a huge one; just a small sign that will verify not merely that you're there, but that you can make things happen at your command. Is it asking so much that You give us something we can really hang on to?"

How we grasp at even the hint of the supernatural: -A dogwood flowering in winter. -An unexplained image in a photo. -An apparition in the night. -A voice heard clearly above our own clanking anxiety. -A car that should have gone over the cliff, but held, dangling as if by an invisible hand. -An unknown man pulling people from a plane, then disappearing. -A dollar bill folded just right to show twin towers...and "OSAMA." Why do we so readily jump to believe these to be manifestations of God or at least the supernatural?

Why? Let's be honest. We so want to verify the presence of an invisible hand, to know once and for all that He IS there. Like the Psalmist, we would like to be vindicated in the eyes of those who scoff at our belief (Ps. 35:23). Along with Thomas, we want to believe in the substance of our own feelings and the reports of others.

There is that longing to examine the reality of God in the same way we verify virtually every other reality. We believe, but how affirming it would be to see and to touch.

We Are the Doubters. We Are the Believers! The apostle John acknowledges this gap in our experience in relating the incident with Thomas. When told that they had seen the Lord, Thomas says he won't believe unless he sees for himself. A week later Jesus appears to Thomas also, and Thomas believes. Jesus' response takes into account the disadvantage we face in not having seen Jesus when He responds to Thomas:

> Have you believed because you have seen Me? Blessed are those have not seen and yet have come to believe. (John 20:29)

Greater faith is required of us than of the apostles. Every one of them saw and touched the Lord, and heard Him speak. Thomas, who had actually seen Jesus perform miracles, refused to take the others' word for it. Why would we NOT want some proof of our belief?

Here we come to the difference between believing and seeing. Belief requires a "leap of faith," a daring to believe in the absence of tangible evidence. It isn't to prove to the doubters as much as to verify our own sense of reality, our own quest to experience God, Who we believe to be with us, Who we believe leads us, and Who we want to love and serve. We believe, but there is so much about God as a spirit that we can't quite explain or verify. We are...if we are honest with ourselves...we are the doubters. At the same time, and more importantly, we are also the believers. Along with Alfred Lord Tennyson we can affirm, "There lives more faith in honest doubt, / Believe me, / than in half the creeds" (*In Memoriam*).

John acknowledges that one of his purposes in writing his Gospel is to promote belief in Jesus as the Messiah. By relating the "signs" performed by Jesus he intends to give credibility to Jesus' claim to being Messiah. He writes,

> Now Jesus did many other signs in the presence of His disciples, which are not written in this book. But these are written so that you may come to believe that Jesus is the Messiah, the Son of God, and that through believing you may have life in His name. (John 20:30-31)

John assumes that what he has written was sufficient to cause a person to believe.

In Peter's first Epistle there is a similar awareness of this dependence on belief, not experience. He writes, "Although you have not seen Him, you love Him; and even though you do not see Him now, you believe in Him and rejoice with an indescribable and glorious joy" (Peter 1:8).

How does a human being make contact with God Who is spirit? If we are to love God, there must be some understanding of how we experience Him. We struggle with this "spiritual dimension" which we know is there. We can't touch it, taste it, hear it, see it, or smell it. We know in our inner self that there is a reality there, but it defies observation and is difficult to quantify.

So we resort to collective historical experience at best, or "putting out the fleece" tests at worst. We associate God with a place, such as church or a mountain retreat. We have our own practices of prayer and contemplation in which we enter into conversation with our heavenly Father. Yet, I repeat, if we are honest with ourselves, there are these questions, this wondering, what is the reality of our experience of God?

Only If It's True. In the beginning scenes of the movie, Dr. Zhivago, a girl is brought before Zhivago's brother, a Russian military commander, who is looking for his niece.. Zhivago had, in the story, become a famous and beloved Russian poet, who is now dead. The commander thinks this girl may be his brother's daughter. He notices that she is carrying a balalaika, a Russian stringed instrument. "My brother played the balalaika," the commander said. "She has a gift," replied the girl's friend. The girl said almost nothing, looking at the man with fear and skepticism. "Don't you want to believe Zhivago is your father," asked the commander?

"Not if it isn't true," she responded.

We want to know if it's true, this belief we have that there is a God, present, but invisible—a Spirit existing in a reality which we feel, sense really, but cannot touch. It isn't a lack of faith that causes us to want to see some visible manifestation of God...at least I don't think it's a lack of faith. For me it's as much a matter of curiosity and a search for understanding as it is of wanting definitive proof. At the same time I must admit to a certain longing to have indisputable evidence.

I'm not even sure how it would change my view of life and humanity if God were to make an unmistakable appearance, which, of course, I believe He did in Jesus His Son. But I was not present to talk with Jesus, to ask Him questions, to see His miracles. My belief is based on what I read of others' experiences in the Bible.

I look at the wondrous varieties of life and find it almost impossible to imagine that life could occur without a Creator. I do see God in magnificent and marvelous life.

In addition, I've experienced God through other people. I attended seminaries and universities for the purpose of experiencing what women and men of faith had discovered about God. I was rewarded with seeing God through their eyes.

Here's the best part. I have seen God most clearly in many people who saw themselves as ordinary, and they were not. I could name so many, would begin but necessarily will resist since I would leave out so many worthy people. I'll name only one, Lois Talbot. She was a great cook. I tasted her artful work many times in the Church where we served together. I'm not going to say she was a saint. I didn't know her that well. But she could cook.

One Sunday she told me the doctor had discovered a malignancy in one of her eyes. She was so frightened. "I don't think I'll be able to drive if they have to remove it," she told me. I went to the hospital to visit her. Unfortunately, the doctors had found it necessary to remove the diseased eye. She smiled bravely when I walked in. I gave her a heart-felt hug and sat down beside her bed. "At least I can still see through my one good eye," she said. "I'm so thankful for that."

I forget what else we talked about, but after I said a prayer she held on to my hand and said, "Larry, I'm so glad you came. I feel like God couldn't come, so He sent you." Oh my goodness! I almost wept but controlled myself because she would have felt she had said something wrong. The truth is that I was the one in the presence of God, and He was this dear woman! I don't think that even God could cook any better than Lois, and I'd just discovered that God couldn't speak any more clearly than in what Lois had said. Only, God didn't send me, alone. He sent Lois. A Godly life such as hers is one of the most powerful realities of the presence of God that we know.

The Human Spirit. Whatever the nature of the spiritual dimension of life, there is a reality to the human spirit that is so strong that humans are willing to die to defend their spiritual values. Making slaves of humans has never been completely successful, for eventually their willingness to die in order to be fully self-determining wins out over those who are unwilling to die to preserve their own control over others. "Give me liberty or give me death" is not only a patriotic cry. It's an intrinsic characteristic of humanity.

Is it a part of the human spirit to want a God to love? Sure, humans have gone through—are still going through—all kinds of different approaches on how to relate to God. All religious expression could be understood as an attempt to satisfy something that is innate in the human spirit. The human spirit longs to understand all reality, including the spiritual reality. The drive to relate to the spiritual dimension causes people to ask what the spiritual "Being" demands or desires of mankind. Does God demand human sacrifices? Would He be satisfied with the product of a man's labor, as in grain or an animal sacrifice instead? Is it possible that the sacrifice He values most is the total devotion to Him and His genuinely benevolent agenda for the world?

What God Wants. Maybe the question isn't so much about what I, or any human, wants or expects from God. What if the world is about what God wants from His creation? If that matters to me it seems I've taken a step beyond mere self-fulfillment and a step towards real love that cares about what God wants. What God wants, in this understanding, is not a robot following a predetermined program—far from that. He wants humanity to develop to its full potential for the sheer joy of being delighted with man's—**man's!**—achievement.

How do we know that to be true? Parents know that one of the greatest satisfactions and affirmations we can receive is in seeing our children accomplish their own goals, fabricate their own creations, and find their own fulfillment. While we may guide, suggest, aid when asked or unobserved, we know well that any attempt to impose on them our own narrow view of their creativity and ability turns out poorly. Okay, God is more knowing than a human parent, but He still chooses to be known as "Father" and not "Dictator." My understanding is that if God insisted on a rigid adherence to His "Plan for my life," He would not take pleasure in a child who accomplished nothing more. The child wouldn't find pleasure in that either. God knows that.

Maybe God wants to know something more. Maybe God wants to know if we love Him, the personal Father, not HIM, the "Wizard Almighty." And He isn't going to tempt us to love Him by bribing us.

Sometimes a husband wants to know his wife loves him enough that she will discern those inner parts of himself and go there—or enough that she will accept him even if she can't know his hidden feelings. Okay, this is a very human way of looking at it, but maybe we got that from God.

Similarly, sometimes a wife wants to hear her husband say he loves her. He might do all the right things—provide financially, do the day-to-day chores a household requires, spend time with their children, and make sacrifices for her. Yet if there is not the expression in words, gestures, and touch, it isn't enough.

I've known a few rich men in my life. Occasionally they have expressed to me the fear that some of their friends don't really love them for themselves. The friends may just love the rich man's money. How could they tell? How can God tell if we love Him, or love only what we can get out of Him?

Love Me—Love My Paintings. I love Vincent Van Gogh's paintings. I can't say I love Vincent. I may very well have found him distasteful or even despised him if given the chance. Not that it occurred to him, or even mattered that I or others might or could have loved or despised him. But I wonder. What would Vincent have chosen—to have someone love his painting—or love him? Oddly, I think it likely that Vincent would have preferred it as it turned out—that he left something to love, namely his paintings. "Vincent" would not endure beyond the lifetime of those who loved him as friend. *VAN GOGH* will exist and be loved for as long as his masterful compositions exist or are remembered. There is a sense in which loving Van Gogh's paintings is loving him...or what mattered about him.

What does God want us to love where He's concerned—Loving Father or all-powerful Wizard? Does He desire that we love Him as painter of flowers and crafter of birds and lions, or our "on a first-name basis" buddy? Existing on a much higher order of awareness than we, does He prefer to be loved for His masterpieces or to be merely loved for His nature, His personality? How does one go about loving a deity?

What does He desire of us?—That we spend our days thinking about Him, singing songs however poorly, endlessly repeating our devotion to Him, talking silently inside our heads to Him, relating all our worries, desires, short-comings, and thoughts? Do gods yawn? Is God pleased when monks and nuns shut themselves up in little cubicles and spend their lives pondering Him? Or, is He more pleased when those same noble men and women devote their lives to caring for suffering people? Each must determine for herself how to love God.

Might it be that He takes the greatest satisfaction in seeing the creation of a Van Gogh, or in listening to the subtleties of a Mozart composition? Does He smile as much at a flippant comment from a drunken Winston Churchill as He does at the passionate, threatening words of a preacher? Did He love Peter less when he whacked off the ear of the servant of the high priest than when Peter came walking to Jesus on the water? Does He prefer Paul when he writes to the Corinthians, "The grace of the Lord Jesus be with you" (1 Cor. 16:23), or what he wrote just before that, "If anyone does not love the Lord—a curse be on him!" (ver. 21)?

Loving Lions. Love is no easy thing. Sometimes I love my wife best when she's lost in her music and I know she isn't thinking about me in the slightest, or when she's doing something really nice for our children or grandchildren.

I think one of the times I was really aware of loving my son was when, at about the age of twelve, I went to see him in the middle of a summer program at a college, missing him dreadfully. At the end of the visit I said to him, "I sure miss having you around." He responded, "Well, you're going to have to miss me again next summer, because I'm coming back here!" So much for mushy sentiment.

Does God like us best when we're getting on with the business of being men and women living the great adventure, drama and risk of life? Does He smile when we get lost in some creative project, or lose our temper when a cruel person harms another? Does God smile and find pleasure when a little kid takes a whack at a bully? And what of the bully? Does God love him too? Of course. Why do we place such a high value on what could be seen as fawning, gratuitous playing to an audience of One?

Okay, I did love it when a dog named Smoky, a beautiful beagle, came running after me one day when out on a walk I dropped his leash—threw it down—when he stubbornly refused to take another step. I hated the time I picked up his crumpled, car-broken body, and took him to the vet who told me his back was broken. I loved Smoky for teaching me that a defiant, mind of his own, spirited animal could make me weep—when no tail-wagging, roll over on his back, tongue-lolling dog ever had.

I've never loved a tiger or a lion or a bear. They aren't that lovable. But then, if they were, they wouldn't be what they are. A bear without a growl just isn't a bear. Go to the zoo, or a circus, sometime and you'll see I'm right.

I've learned a great deal from a man who once called me a liar. Gruff, profane, cantankerous, and a once troublesome neighbor, we now enjoy a glass of holiday cheer every Christmas. I don't think I would enjoy him nearly as much if he didn't bark and sometimes bite. It's said that "Man's chief end is to glorify God, and to enjoy Him for ever" (The Westminster Shorter Catechism). If that's so, (and I think that, properly understood, it's true) who gets to determine what "glorifying God" is? I think God loves wolves as much as He loves basset hounds, and sharks as much as He loves porpoises. I think God admired "Give 'em hell" Harry Truman as much as the Scripture quoting Jimmy Carter.

So you see, this matter of loving God just isn't that simple. Easy enough to say, "You shall love the Lord your God with all your heart, soul, mind and strength," but, oh my, please tell me what that means. Show me God and then I'll figure out how to love Him. This invisible God is a little hard to get my arms around. Yet there is this unquenchable belief within that it is possible to get my arms around Him, or at least the arms of my spirit. The spirit within me reaches out to "The Spirit" which I believe to be around me, and which sometimes is felt as an overwhelming reality within me. But that's just it—it's my reality and I can't reproduce it in a laboratory for you or anybody else. You'll just have to be your own laboratory of experiencing the Spirit of God...if you choose.

My desire is to urge other people to seek that reality...not to impose my reality on them, but for them to learn of their own spiritual reality if they have the desire. In that way I hope to expand my own spiritual reality. The Spirit of God, as I understand it, is far too vast for any one human to experience totally. I cannot even think about loving the Lord my God with all my heart without recognizing that for me it is a partial, limited, but oh so incredibly brilliant facet of the human experience.

The Idea of God. I asked two people with whom I was having breakfast if they loved God. The man said, "Yes, I love God." The woman said, "I hope I love God." For most of the years of my life I would have responded as the man. "Certainly, I love God. Why would you even think to ask such a question?" I pushed further—What does it mean to you that you love God? The man's answer took the direction of the things he sees that he attributes to God...the birth of babies, the blessings of his life, and all of the ways he sees God at work in his life. I could relate very well and it felt good to hear him affirm some of my own feelings.

I asked the woman why she said she "hoped" she loved God. She said, "Maybe I love the 'idea' of God, and I hope there is a reality beyond that idea." *To love the idea of God* may give us a clue as to what it means to love God. To love someone is to be aware that there exists outside of myself something that would diminish me if it did not exist.

In the fictional book, The Story of Pi, a boy tells of his adventure at sea stranded on a raft with a tiger. Later he is being interviewed and a man asks him if he really expects them to believe he survived for weeks on a raft, alone with a tiger. He responded by asking them whether they liked the story better with or without the tiger?

For me, it's not so much liking the story of life better with God than without. It's more that life and the world make more sense with God than without. I would feel diminished without God as a part of my awareness. I imagine that an actual appearance by the Creator would broaden my awareness. Maybe I couldn't handle it. Nevertheless, I keep looking for evidence of His presence as I would keep an eye open for a glimpse of one I love.

Keeping His Commandments. When I asked one man if he loved God he responded that he wasn't even sure he believed in God. He continued:

> I try to live a godly life. I believe it is the right way to live, the best way. I believe in the moral values taught by most

religions. I think Jesus was one of the greatest men that ever lived and His teaching that we are to have compassion for everyone is the most important thing for all people. Jesus is the best example I know. I ask, "What would Jesus do?" When I look at people in the street, I wonder if that's Jesus there. I think that's how Jesus wanted us to think.

Is it possible that adhering to what we perceive to be Godly values is a form of loving God, even without knowing it? Jesus said, "If you love me you will keep my commandments." Is the reverse true as well—"If you keep my commandments you love me?" On another occasion He said, "Not everyone who says to Me, 'Lord, Lord,' will enter the kingdom of heaven, but only he who does the will of My Father Who is in heaven" (Matt. 7:21). Entrance into the kingdom is determined by actions, not by words.

A woman who had heard me talking about my quest to understand what it meant to love God said to me, "The answer is easy." She then quoted the statement of Jesus that if we love Him we will keep His commandments (Jn. 14:15). I replied that I didn't think it was that simple. However, given all that is said about doing the will of God or Jesus it is evident that "keeping His commandments" is a very significant part of loving God. It might even be the most important part.

My hesitancy in embracing the idea of equating keeping the commandments with loving the Father is based on the motive for one's keeping the commandments. I've known people who have been very rigid in their practice of observing the commandments, yet their hearts seem out of tune with God. I'm reminded of Jesus accusing the Pharisees of honoring God with their lips but their hearts being far from Him.

There was a time in my own life when I was convinced that obeying the commandments was the key to entering heaven. My conviction was flawed, however, as it demanded obeying according to MY understanding. I think I can say that whatever love for God was present in my life at that time, my devotion to my legalistic view of following God was greater than my love for God. I mistook my zeal for my views as love for God. The two are not the same.

In the last section of this book I will deal with what the Scriptures teach about our loving God. My journey with God began with careful attention to Scripture, as I understood it as a child. In this middle section I have pursued my adult ponderings about how loving God helps in understanding life and the world God created. Finally, I wish to look at Scripture again through eyes experienced by my wondrous journey through life

PART III
Love In The Bible

IX.
God's Love for Man in Genesis

We twenty-first century people are not the first to try to figure out God. From the studies of anthropologists we know that the earliest humans had ideas about gods and rituals for interacting with their gods. Whatever our religion, we humans have a long history of trying to understand God.

The community of faith in which I have experienced and learned of God has a rich history which informs my own understanding of God. In this final section I offer observations on this history and approach to God which I embrace and in which I believe. The Bible is my primary book of faith, a record of the experiences many women and men had with God. It's the guide for my life and the foundation of knowing what it means to love God.

Why Should God Care About Man? How is it that God, the creator of the universe, came to love mankind? Why should beings so inferior to God matter to Him at all? Human endeavors must seem so trivial to One Who is able to speak worlds into existence. Or are they?

Is it possible that the great drama of our world brings great satisfaction—or disappointment—to our Creator? Does God look on the unfolding drama of human history as an anxious parent watching her children find their way? Does God participate with us in ways hidden from our view or difficult for us to understand?

These are the same questions posed by the Psalmist who asks:

What are human beings that You are mindful of them, mortals that You care for them? (Ps. 8:4)

The Psalmist's answer reflects some of the same thoughts given in the first chapter of Genesis:

Yet You have made them a little lower than God, and crowned them with glory and honor. You have given them dominion over the works of Your hands; You have put all things under their feet, all sheep and oxen, and also the beasts of the field, the birds of the air, and the fish of the sea, whatever passes along the paths of the seas. (Ps. 8:5-8 Cf. Gen. 1:26 ff.)

For us it's a question of scale. Can a man love an ant? I have enjoyed watching ants at work. I've been amazed at the teamwork of a colony of ants. If I had created the ants, I might find real pleasure in their ingenuity and resourcefulness. But love? It just doesn't work. Ants might make good science projects, but you'd never make a pet of one.

So, how can God love man? Through the centuries, those who ponder God have concluded that He does. We don't have to know how or why. The Bible merely affirms that He does. Let's look at how the ancient account of the beginning of the world explains this loving relationship between God and man.

In God's Image. It isn't surprising that the very first book of the Bible deals with our insecurity about our own inadequacy where God is concerned. As the crowning achievement to His creation God says, "Let Us make humankind in Our image, according to Our likeness..." (Gen. 1:26). As if sensing humankind's reticence to accept this assessment it is repeated in the next verse, not once, but twice: "So God created humankind in His image, in the image of God He created them; male and female He created them" (1:27). Note that women are created in the image of God as well as men, a reference to the female image of God—a fact that should not be overlooked.

What is this image of God in which we are created? Understanding God begins with taking a look at ourselves. There is something God-like about us, something that reflects Who He is. Since He is not physical the likeness must not be in the human form. If that were so, then it could also be said that apes were created, however poorly, in the image of God. The image must be in human nature, in human capability and understanding.

The Genesis accounts of creation do not tell us that God loved humankind, but they do indicate the highest regard of God for man. The honor of imprinting His image on humankind is followed up by statements that the earth is created for the purpose of providing a suitable place for humankind to thrive. God blesses humankind and tells them to fill the earth and subdue it. He gives them dominion over all creation, after which He says, "See, I have given you every plant yielding seed that is upon the face of all the earth, and every tree with seed in its fruit; you shall have them for food" (1:29). This is reinforced in the words that God provides all manner of plants which are "pleasant to the sight and good for food" (2:9).

There is no reason given for God's astonishing deed in creating man in His likeness, and then bestowing on humankind the magnificent gift of the entire earth. There is not in the creation account any statement of God having love for His creation or humankind. Creation pleases Him as seen in His assessment, "it is very good" (1:31). From all of this we can only conclude that God cares very much for man, and the whole of creation, but it's not stated.

Here in the idyllic setting of the garden earth God imposes only one condition on humankind. He commands that they not eat of the tree of the knowledge of good and evil (2:17). Implied in this command is the intent that humankind shall remain naïve and innocent. While they have dominion over all the earth, they don't have the ability to discern good from evil, except where the tree is concerned. If they eat of it, they die. Their consciousness is like that of other living beings. Yet there is a difference. The consciousness of the animals is apparently not honored by this command, this restriction on eating from that one tree. The implication is that there is no ability on the part of the animals to attain wisdom or knowledge, while humankind is pregnant with the possibility of becoming more than what first meets the eye.

This difference is expressed in the fruit being desired by the woman to "make one wise." The animals are not capable of such a desire. This prompts the question, at what point does sentient life make the leap to being capable of knowledge and wisdom? I do not propose to answer that question, but somewhere in the answer is bound up the potential that man has, not only to obey, but also to love. This potential is recognized in God's giving commands only to humankind.

God states that the difference in man before and after eating the fruit is that "the man has become like one of us, knowing good and evil" (3:22). Is **that** the difference between humans and the other animals? It is a significant difference, but does it reflect merely a difference in intelligence, or is their some other higher level of awareness? Does being sentient come down to "knowing good and evil?"

Man's Quest for God. Humankind has this special characteristic of being able to make moral decisions about their actions. Thus, the command not to eat of the tree of the knowledge of good and evil can be imposed on humans, but is apparently unnecessary for other animals. It acknowledges the higher order of awareness possessed by humankind. Humankind needs moral guidance and God gives it.

Is this giving of commands a demonstration of God's love? The Psalmist believes it is, writing: "Deal with your servant according to your steadfast love, and teach me your statutes" (Ps. 119:124). Seventeen times the Psalmist speaks of his love for God's name and God's steadfast love. Ten times reference is made to the delight brought by God's commands. God's love for humans is demonstrated by His giving commands to humankind.

Commands are not the only interaction between God and humans. Upon Adam and Eve's disobeying the command about the tree, God expresses His displeasure by increasing the woman's pain in childbirth and imposing hard labor on man. Adam and Eve are banished from the Garden, indicating a breech between them and God that results from their disobedience. This sets the stage for humankind attempting to restore the lost relationship and God setting the conditions of that restoration.

Significantly, after God punishes Adam and Eve, humankind begins to search for ways to please God. Without being commanded to do so, both Cain and Abel bring offerings to God. Why would

Cain or Able think it appropriate to give God what they had produced by their own efforts? They have labored, as a result of their parent's disobedience, to produce grain and flocks. The penalty of toil and sweat has fallen on them as well as their parents. There is no indication that God has asked for any offering.

Putting aside the question of why one offering was accepted and the other rejected, it's interesting that the humans bring to God something for which He has no need. Yes, it is a sacrifice for them, but a sacrifice that is of no benefit to God. When one offering is accepted and the other rejected, the giver of the rejected gift becomes "angry, and his countenance fell" (Gen. 4:5). In the absence of any other explanation this rejection by God may be interpreted not as punishment but as God offering direction to humankind. At the very least He communicates that animal offerings are pleasing while grain offerings are not. It could be further implied that God wanted these first humans to be shepherds, not farmers. (This view is echoed by John Steinbeck in his book, *East of Eden*, in which he gives an excellent treatment of this subject.)

Whether these early attempts by humans to please God were out of fear or thankfulness cannot be determined with certainty. Since the gifts are seemingly spontaneous we can assume they were a thankful recognition of God's blessings—an overflowing joy, the first celebration of Thanksgiving Day! There seems to be no attempt on the part of the writer to acknowledge any feelings of love or even affection between God and humankind. We can only deduce from the actions of each that there was a budding affection for each other.

What Will Man Become? There is also a sense that each does not know what to expect of the other. God, for His part, has deliberately created a being that is unpredictable. It's not helpful to speculate as to whether God knows what humans are going to do before they do it. Could He? Perhaps, but that isn't the point. He creates animals so that whatever they do, it isn't a thought-out moral decision. He creates man with the capability of reasoning, but along with reasoning the freedom to make the choice to go against reason. God allows humankind the very god-like ability to become their own being, their own self, to have their own nature. That is the very essence of being created in the image of God.

Humankind, on the other hand, does not know the nature of God except for what they see in His creation and what they can sense in themselves. They disobey His one command and see that failing to heed His instruction leads to separation from Him, and to a more difficult and painful life. Now in the absence of the tree of the knowledge of good and evil they are left, apparently, to figure out His wishes, "the rules," on their own with only hints given as to whether He is pleased or not.

In attempting to express appreciation they learn that God will react with regard for one offering but not for the other. How God expresses this regard we are not told. It's possible that it's expressed in an increase to Abel's flock and a decrease in Cain's success in farming. People still often view success as an indication of God's goodwill and failure as His displeasure. I'm not so sure. That wasn't true for Job. It also didn't turn out that way for Jesus, at least not at the end of His lifetime.

This view of good fortune as an expression of God's goodwill is reinforced when Eve gives birth to her third son, Seth. Her response is, "God has appointed for me another child instead of Abel, because Cain killed him" (4:25). She interprets her joy to be the favor of God.

Invoking the Name of the Lord. Upon the birth of Seth's first son, Enosh, a new behavior is introduced. "At that time people began to invoke the name of the Lord" (4:26). How remarkable that in the interim since the creation of Adam the connection between God and man is so nebulous. No explanation of "invoking the name of the Lord" is given. The phrase implies a welcomed and expectant acknowledgement of God's presence. It is different from God's speaking earlier to Adam and Eve and Cain, and does not seem to imply a direct reply from God. Invoking or calling on the name of the Lord continues with Abraham and his descendants.

Note that there is a pause in God's speaking to people between Cain and Noah. This could be seen as a time when the descendants of Eve were aware of God's existence but during which time there was no direct communication. Enoch is singled out for having "walked with God" (4:22-24), without any explanation of what that meant. Humankind multiplies in the period between Seth and Noah, but there is little that is reported. It's perhaps a time for God to observe what will become of humankind. Will they develop in a way that pleases Him or will they become a disappointment?

By the time of Noah the assessment was not favorable:

The Lord saw that the wickedness of humankind was great in the earth, and that every inclination of the thoughts of their hearts was only evil continually. And the Lord was sorry that He had made humankind on the earth, and it grieved Him to His heart. (6:5, 6)

The expression, "grieved Him to His heart," indicates a deep sense of caring along with the disappointment. As the creator of humankind He had anticipated satisfaction at what they would become. Instead, they have brought deep sorrow. His caring for humankind—one might say that His love for His creation—is expressed in His sorrow at their thoughts and evil deeds.

God's dealings with humankind have been limited to this point. Certainly the creation event, including the lavish provisions made for Adam and Eve, indicates how important humankind was to God. Other than the simple commandment forbidding the fruit of the one tree, there are few instructions provided. Humankind is given dominion over the whole world and the implication is that they are to figure out how to subdue it—to take care of it for their own benefit.

It turns out that they are not content to simply live out their lives in this dominant role, with awareness superior to the animals yet falling short of having God-like knowledge and awareness. This is the point of God's statement after the eating of the fruit, when He says, "See, the man has become like one of Us, knowing good and evil; and now, he might reach out his hand and take also from the tree of life, and eat, and live forever" (3:22). Is it possible that God's concern is not that humankind will become His rival, but that they will reach a stage when they simply have no use for Him? They won't care whether He's there or not? He'll become unnecessary to them? Does that sound familiar? That would ruin everything God had set out to accomplish.

An End to Ambiguity. After the "Fall" the encounters between God and humankind provide little guidance as to how they are to relate to each other. There is an ambiguity in what they expect from each other. Cain commits murder after both he and Abel attempt to approach God with an offering. The ultimate outcome is that first, God has regard for animal sacrifices and, second, God is very upset with murder. No command is given. It isn't needed after God chastises and curses Cain. The point is taken—don't murder other humans. It brings down the curse of God.

Eve gives God the credit for the birth of Seth but there is no stated interaction between her and God. Enoch walks with God, which implies a relationship, but one that leaves us yearning for a deeper understanding of what that means.

It comes then as almost a relief when God finally states how He's feeling about the way humankind is developing. The assessment is ominous, but at least mankind knows God has not forgotten about His creation, and that He's not disinterested. He's still looking in, though as of yet He's not intervened. How are they to know if He will?

From God's point of view humans have made a mess of things on their own. He has provided the most beautiful and supportive surroundings they could want. They mistakenly come to see the world as existing for their pleasure alone. They spend their inheritance in riotous living. Even if they don't recognize it, they are not the final *determinators* of what earth will become. God determines to destroy the entire project.

However, among the ruins of this once glorious garden world is found one man and his family who are still getting it right. Evil is all around, but Noah finds favor in God's eyes. The interaction between him and God sets the stage for how God interacts with humans thereafter. Namely, God proposes some seemingly preposterous action, as in telling Noah to build the ark, and the person accepts it as a divine imperative. These propositions are different from commands. They are God shaping a person through promising them a successful outcome to adventuresome but seemingly impossible missions.

Consider the examples in the adventure ahead:
– God tells Noah to build a huge boat on land because a flood is coming.
– God tells Abraham to pull up stakes and go to a land he's never seen.
– Moses tells Pharaoh to release his Hebrew slaves.
– David dares to face a giant with only a sling.
– Jesus accepts His mission to willingly die on a cross.
– Christians accept that God will make the seemingly impossible possible.

Noah Restarts Humankind. The story of Noah is well-known. Quite simply put, Noah does what God tells him to do (Gen, 6:22). Because of this he is seen as "righteous" (7:1). When the flood recedes the first thing that Noah does is to build an altar to the Lord and offer burnt offerings (8:20). There is no statement that God tells him to do this. It may be a remembering from Abel's example. The outcome is good. The odor is pleasing to God, resulting in His making a new covenant with Noah, all mankind and with every living creature.

Included in the covenant are both promises and commandments. The promises are similar to those given to Adam. In addition, God states that He will never again destroy the earth with water. The rainbow is the sign of that promise. There are two commandments. The first forbids the eating of blood. The second forbids the shedding of the blood of another human. Times were simple then (Gen. 9:4-6).

There is a bond formed between God and Noah as a result of the flood. Noah merits God's guidance and protection because he is a righteous man. Beyond that he has followed what must seem to him strange instructions in building the ark. God has explained to him that He is going to destroy the earth, but that must have seemed improbable to Noah. It is said of Noah, as it had been said of Enoch, that he walked with God. With Noah we see walking with God includes taking guidance from God and following His instructions.

After the flood, Noah's spontaneous building of the altar is rewarded with the blessing of God, a promise that life will go well for Noah. Noah acknowledges his dependence upon God for direction in uncertain times. God demonstrates His caring for Noah in guiding him and then blessing him when he follows. Here we have a sense of the kind of relationship God had hoped for when He created humankind. Adam and Eve disappointed God in their failure to follow His command. It was nevertheless a beginning. Noah takes the next step by trusting God even though it didn't seem reasonable.

The Call of Abraham. It's Noah's descendant Abraham who advances this relationship begun by Noah. Residing in a fertile region in the area of the Tigris-Euphrates Rivers, Abraham draws God's attention—for no reason that we are given. Noah gains God's attention by his righteousness. God's favor on Abraham actually begins with his father, Terah. It is Terah who first sets out for Canaan (11:31), taking his family with him. For some reason when he reaches Haran he settles there, short of his goal.

After Terah's death God says to Abraham, "Go to the land I will show you" (12:1ff.). The text doesn't give us details of how God spoke to Abraham, whether in words Abraham heard, in a dream, or simply in Abraham's awareness in his own mind. He knew his father had set off for Canaan but had stopped short in Haran. Was there implanted in Abraham's mind a fascination with Canaan, a carry-over from his father's dream? Does God sometimes plant the seed in the father and have it sprout in the child? I think it probable.

I can relate to this possibility in my own experience. In my father's stories of Colorado that he related to his children in bedtime stories there was planted a fascination with the West, which remains with me to this day. It may have been of some influence in causing me to make an improbable decision to leave a cushy position on the East coast and go to an unknown situation in Arizona. I can't say that God spoke to me in making that decision. I can say that there was a sense of God's direction in the decision. I can also say that God has blessed me and my family in Arizona. I wonder if that's how it was for Abraham?

On the other hand, I must also acknowledge that I believe God would have blessed me in New Jersey had I made the decision to stay there. There were wonderful people there who encouraged me to stay. However, I didn't have the sense that New Jersey was where God was calling me.

Abraham is the beginning of not merely one man's lifetime relationship with God, but of a nation's relationship with God, a relationship that has endured for several thousand years. God promises Abraham that He will make of him a great nation, and that all families on earth will be blessed in him (12:2, 3). Abraham departed, not knowing where he would end up, but believing he would be shown the land where God wanted him to become that nation.

In the subsequent events of Abraham's life we see ups and downs, starts and stops, good and bad, with Abraham sometimes displaying remarkable confidence in God's leading. At other times Abraham completely fails to trust God to take care of him. As his descendant, Joseph, would later say to his brothers, speaking of both the good and the bad, "Even though you intended to do harm to me, God intended it for good, in order to preserve a numerous people, as He is doing today" (50:20). It is that assurance that has continued to define the relationship between God and His people. It's expressed by the Apostle Paul when he writes, "We know that all things work together for good for those who love God, who are called according to His purpose" (Rom. 8:28).

Observe that to this point in Genesis the word love has not been used, not even once. This is not to say it did not yet exist among humans, but it seems at least ironic in our quest to discover the substance of love between God and humankind that in the accounts of the early experiences of humans with God the word "love" isn't even mentioned.

The First Use of the Word "Love" in Genesis. With Abraham the word "love" is introduced in a most extraordinary way. The very first occurrence is in the words of God to Abraham: "Take your son, your only son Isaac, **whom you love**, and go to the land of Moriah, and offer him there as a burnt offering on one of the mountains that I shall show you" (22:2). Two things seize our attention. First, as Christians, we cannot help but notice the symbolic connection between what God asks of Abraham, "Take your son, your only son," and what God himself does centuries later with His own Son.

Second, the significance of God's words, "whom you love," cannot be overemphasized for our study. Abraham has reason to cherish this son more than usual. He's the child of his old age, his only son by his wife, Sarah. He's trusted that God would provide a son, an heir. God had promised. To ask Abraham now, not only to give Isaac up, but also to sacrifice him with his own hand is outrageous. Few people will have their love for God tested to this extreme.

What is it that God is testing? On the surface it seems God is testing Abraham's obedience. The text doesn't say that God was testing Abraham's love for Him, but love is the word that is used for Abraham's feelings toward Isaac. It seems clear that God is forcing Abraham to sort out how much he loves Isaac and how much he loves God. "Abraham, do you love Me more than you love your son?" That isn't stated but it's right in the middle of what is being asked.

It's possible that for Abraham there was a parallel question of, do you trust Me more than you trust your own reason? We can't say, but what we know is that Abraham was ready to carry out the action. He's poised to kill his son when the angel stops him.

The question could also be, "Do you fear Me more than you dread sacrificing your son?" In fact, the words of the angel upon stopping Abraham from killing Isaac are, "for now I know that you fear God, since you have not withheld your son, your only son, from Me" (22:12). The action preceding these words gives a new dimension to the word fear. Almost any parent would have responded to God's command to sacrifice his child by saying, "Kill me if you must, but let my child live."

No, the inescapable conclusion is that Abraham loves God enough to sacrifice all that is dear to him. It's not fear of the consequences. It's more than blind trust. It's complete devotion to the

One, the only One, Who deserves it. In being willing to offer his son, Abraham demonstrates that he loves God more than he loves his son, himself, or anyone, or anything else. Thus understood, this first occurrence of the word love gives us a dramatic illustration of what it ultimately means for a person to love God.

This is a most extraordinary test of love, but there are others that are related to it. Scripture contains many variations. Jesus says, "No one has greater love than this, to lay down one's life for one's friends" (Jn. 15:13). This statement follows immediately His commandment to His disciples, "that you love one another as I have loved you" (v. 12).

Second Occurrence of "Love" in Genesis. In concluding this examination of God's developing relationship to humankind in Genesis we look at the second occurrence of the word love in Genesis. It also involves Abraham's son, Isaac. It's spoken by Abraham's servant as he carries out Abraham's request that he find a wife from his kin for his son, Isaac. Standing outside the town where Abraham's kinfolk live, the servant prays to God for guidance in selecting the right woman:

> O LORD, God of my master Abraham, please grant me success today and show **steadfast love** to my master Abraham. I am standing here by the spring of water, and the daughters of the townspeople are coming out to draw water. Let the girl to whom I shall say, 'Please offer your jar that I may drink,' and who shall say, 'Drink, and I will water your camels'—let her be the one whom You have appointed for Your servant Isaac. By this I shall know that You have shown **steadfast love** to my master. (24:12-14)

When the girl, Rebekah, behaves in the manner specified by the servant, he thanks God and says,

> Blessed be the LORD, the God of my master Abraham, Who has not forsaken his **steadfast love** and His faithfulness toward my master. As for me, the LORD has led me on the way to the house of my master's kin. (24:27)

The fact that the servant speaks of God's "steadfast love" three times clearly shows that the concept of God's loving Abraham is well known in Abraham's household. The servant's prayer also demonstrates that God's love extends not only to Abraham but includes those of his household who pray to Him, as we see in the servant's words that, "the Lord has led me on the way."

An Umbrella of Love. A reading of the book of Genesis provides us with a picture of the developing relationship between God and humankind, especially those Who He selects to be His people. This is not to say that God does not also love all other people. He specifically protects and blesses Ishmael, promising to "make him a great nation (17:20-21). Melchizedek, King of Salem and named as a priest "of God Most High," receives from Abraham one-tenth of his possessions. Melchizedek offers up his own blessing on Abraham and also God. We assume that the household of Melchizedek had experienced the love of God.

There's an additional dimension to God's love for humankind that's worth noting. In each of the repetitions of God's covenant with Abraham there's the promise that "all the families of the earth shall be blessed" (12:3 *et al.*). This is given an added dimension in Abraham's bargaining with God over the inhabitants of Sodom and Gomorrah. Abraham asks God if He would "slay the righteous with the wicked, so that the righteous fare as the wicked!" The Lord replies, "If I find at Sodom fifty righteous in the city, I will forgive the whole place for their sake" (18:25, 26). This is a stunning revelation that God will spare the numerous wicked for the sake of the few righteous. God's love extends to the righteous wherever they are found.

The importance of a community of faith loving God is seen in its implications for blessing all people everywhere. I believe it's important for righteous people to love God on behalf of humankind. While they secure His blessings for themselves they also cover the whole earth with the protective umbrella of God's love. Jesus acknowledges this when He says, "Love your enemies and pray for those who persecute you, so that you may be children of your Father in heaven; for He makes His sun rise on the evil and on the good, and sends rain on the righteous and on the unrighteous" (Matt. 5:44,45). The children of God are to love their enemies, just as does their heavenly Father.

The book of Genesis raises interesting questions about what man has become, and what man will become. Humankind doesn't happily settle down in the garden earth, even the Garden of Eden, and live happily ever after. There's no earthly "happily ever after" for humankind, a final blissful state of man's relationship with God. There is only the next horizon, the next summit, and the next obstacle to be overcome. When humankind ceases to attempt new and bold objectives and settles down in some supposedly perfect garden, the human spirit will dwindle, will go to seed. Hopefully a new seed sprouts and a new direction is taken which leads to some great new human adventure, some new accomplishment.

X.
Love to a Thousand Generations

The Developing Love Between God and Humankind. Following the creation accounts in Genesis, God's love for His people is mentioned hundreds of times in the Bible. It's hard to count the exact number of occurrences but it's a major theme. The expression, "His love endures forever" occurs forty-one times. God's "unfailing love" is mentioned thirty-two times. Oddly, the love of man for God is expressed less than half as frequently as the love of God for His people. Again and again Scripture affirms that God loves His people with an enduring and unfailing love.

I do not find it surprising that a major theme of the Bible is that God loves man, enduringly and unfailingly. "Enduringly" describes the tenacity of God's love as compared to the fickleness of man. "Unfailingly" speaks to the power of His love to provide what His people need to fulfill their humanity. Nevertheless, the question from the previous chapter as to why God would love man remains unanswered.

The simple reality is that God does love man. It's not a matter of logic. It's a matter of love. It's just the way it is. I perhaps accepted it more readily as a child. It was so reassuring to know that the One Who gave me life also loved me, personally. He provided for me, watched over me and guided me. How easily I accepted His engulfing favor and care. It made life like a sweet inviting meadow on a warm summer day. It made even of winter a fairyland of snow and ice given for my enjoyment. The beautiful world was God's gift to me because He loved me.

I knew that God loved me because I had been taught that He did. From the time I knew anything about the Bible, the words of John, "For God so loved the world that He gave His only Son..." were words by which I lived. I inherited that awareness. What of those who didn't have the benefit of those or similar words? How would they know that God loved them?

Man's Awareness of God's Love. The awareness that God loved humankind must have developed gradually. It slips through under the radar screen of the book of Genesis. If God told Adam or Noah or Abraham that He loved them the words are not recorded in Scripture. However, Abraham knew it, as we learned in a statement by his oldest and most trusted servant.

It's doubtful that the servant had come to this idea of God showing steadfast love to Abraham on his own. We can only conclude that he learned it from Abraham. It seems remarkable that God's love is not mentioned earlier, perhaps in one of the blessings God pronounces on Abraham. Abraham had somehow come to know that God loved him, but perhaps it wasn't something he talked about openly.

Twice more God's love for the descendents of Abraham is mentioned, first by Jacob, Isaac's son who is fearful that his brother Esau will kill him. He prays that God will deliver him from Esau, acknowledging, "I am not worthy of the least of all the steadfast love and all the faithfulness that You have shown to Your servant" (Gen. 32:10).

Esau spares Jacob, who becomes the father of twelve sons. One of the sons, Joseph, becomes the victim of his brothers' jealousy and is sold into slavery in Egypt. In Egypt Joseph is falsely accused by his master's wife and is thrown into prison. The writer observes that, "the LORD was with Joseph and showed him steadfast love" (Gen. 39:21). This is the third and last instance in which God's love is mentioned in Genesis.

We cannot say that God's love for His people is not significant in Genesis. It just isn't spelled out clearly. God's favor is indicated by His prospering those whom He chooses. Neither the love of God for man nor the love of man for God is elaborated upon. Yet it is evident in such instances as Noah's being spared during the flood, Abraham's willingness to sacrifice his son, and even in the first offerings of Cain and Abel.

God restores Joseph to favor. During a famine his father, Jacob, now called "Israel," and the entire family is given land in Egypt. Sanctuary in Egypt turns out to be a mixed blessing as it is followed by their becoming slaves to the Egyptians. This accounts for the need for God to deliver the children of Israel from Egypt.

Moses arrives on the scene and becomes the reluctant instrument of God in leading the Israelites out of Egypt. God tells him to announce to the people, "I will redeem you with an outstretched arm and with mighty acts of judgment" (Ex. 6:6). God promises that the Israelites will be His people and He will give them a land (6:1-8). This promise of redemption becomes the ultimate expression of God's love for His people throughout history.

Upon being released by Pharaoh the Israelites cross the Red Sea. In celebration, a song is composed telling how God has delivered

His people from Egypt by leading them through the Red Sea on dry ground. The song gives us the first statement in Scripture of God's loving the entire nation of Israel. The statement is, "In Your unfailing love You will lead the people You have redeemed. In Your strength You will guide them to Your holy dwelling" (Ex. 15:13). The evidence of God's love for His people is seen not merely in His mighty acts of confounding their enemies, but also in His leading. As stated here, the goal of that leading is to bring them to His holy dwelling, which we understand to be the Promised Land and the Temple.

God had led His people before. Noah was led to build an ark and thus survive the flood. Abraham was led to leave Ur of the Chaldeans to go to a land God would show him. There he was led in many ways, as were his offspring. Abraham's servant acknowledges that God has led him on his journey to find a wife for Isaac. The word "redemption" does not occur until in connection with freeing His people from the bondage and oppression in Egypt. It is at this point that the concept of the leading of God expands to include the entire nation.

Man's Love for God—First Occurrence. At last we come to a statement of the importance of man's love for God. It occurs in a most unusual place. It's included in the context of a perplexing statement about the enduring consequences of sin. The first commandment, as it is elaborated, contains the first occurrence of how important it is for humankind to love God.

> And God spoke all these words: "I am the LORD your God, Who brought you out of Egypt, out of the land of slavery. You shall have no other gods before Me. You shall not make

for yourself an idol in the form of anything in heaven above or on the earth beneath or in the waters below. You shall not bow down to them or worship them; for I, the LORD your God, am a jealous God, punishing the children for the sin of the fathers to the third and fourth generation of those who hate Me, but showing love to a thousand generations of those who love Me and keep My commandments." (Ex. 20:1-6)

The commandment in itself does not require love. "You shall have no other gods before Me," is simply a demand, a condition, upon which the relationship between God and His people depends. It could be obeyed without love. However, it cannot be disobeyed without destroying the covenant. If all the other commandments are kept except this one, there is no covenant. This is the one, unconditional requirement upon which a relationship with God rests.

This is not to say that the other commandments are negotiable or situational. However, the other commandments can be broken and forgiveness is possible. Forgiveness is not possible so long as there is allegiance at any level to another god. One could say that the first and foremost requirement for loving God is making Him your one and only God.

Love to a Thousand Generations. In this reference to the love of God and man for each other there is a disproportionate scale of consequences that is easily overlooked. Punishment is not to be the dominant element in God's dealing with His people. "Showing love" is His long-range promise...and a good thing, given the fact that His people so often turn away from Him. This passage foreshadows the necessity of repeated forgiveness on the part of God Who would dare to love man.

What I have heard and read most is that the sins of the father will result in the punishment of his children for three or four generations. I have talked with parents who are concerned that their sins will continue to bring God's punishment to their children through their great-great grandchildren.

That view is very out of balance. The threat of punishment to the children of those who hate God is limited to the third and fourth generation. Compare that with the love to a thousand generations of those who love God and keep His commandments! What a contrast in consequences! For hating God there will be punishment for three or four generations. Yet the love of one ancestor for God brings God's love to their children for a thousand generations—in other words, almost without end. The scales tip heavily to the side of those who love God, even if they are guilty of sin—and who isn't?

This is a defining moment in the thought of the children of Israel, and for all of us who have inherited the Jewish view of God. Yes, there is a forward reaching punishment that comes from hating God, but there is an overwhelming and almost endless blessing that follows those who love God.

God's Disproportionate Memory. This all-powerful, not to be resisted, God has a memory of those who resist Him, but it's very short compared to His memory of those who love Him. His memory is dominated by any show of love from His people. How we misunderstand the demands of God when we focus on His punishment. It's nothing compared to His favor on those who make every effort to love Him.

Notice here two shifts. First, there is the subtle shift from the "bull-dozing" love of God that tolerates no resistance, to the enduring love of God that continues for more than one moment in time. Ah, but second, there is the new element that He desires to be loved in return! There it is, and it's the basis of the question I am attempting to answer—How do we go about loving God?

Occurring as it does, as a part of the first commandment, the implication is that what it means to love God is to keep His commandments. They are to become the focus of the person who loves God. Indeed, this became the focus of many of the religious leaders for centuries. The idea persists today, that a relationship with God consists primarily in obeying His commands. This usually occurs in reference to a select group of commands and how they are to be carried out correctly.

Hear O Israel—Love the Lord Your God. It is not rigid obedience that denotes love. This concept is presented as Moses reviews the law in what has become known as the Shema (Hebrew for "hear"). Prior to entering the Promised Land Moses reminds the people of the events that have happened during their wandering in the wilderness. They have heard the voice of God and seen His presence at Mt. Sinai, something no other people, not even their children, would see. Loving God includes more than seeing and hearing Him, and more than observing His commands. This is what Moses says:

> Hear, O Israel: The LORD is our God, the LORD alone. You shall love the LORD your God with all your heart, and with all your soul, and with all your might. Keep these words that I am commanding you today in your heart. (Deut. 6:4-6)

This restatement of the law by Moses seems to add a new understanding—the awareness of a new dimension, implicit in the first version of the commandment, but not clearly stated. The first commandment is, "You shall have no other gods before Me." This is followed in the first Exodus account with the commentary that God "shows love to a thousand generations of those who love Me and keep My commandments." Note Moses' observation, "Keep these words...in your heart."

Laws, even God's laws, were never intended to remain in stone. If they were we'd have the original tablets given to Moses. By the way, almost everyone would agree that the stones themselves probably contained only abbreviations of the commandments such as: I. No other Gods. II. No Idols. III. Lord's Name Holy. IV. Sabbath.... If they had been as detailed as even the Exodus 20 account has them, someone would have preserved them exactly in writing.

The great commandment was never written in stone. "Loving God" was intended to be inscribed on the more enduring and meaningful medium of human hearts. Keeping the commandments was never intended to be separate from loving God. Loving God is far more inclusive and demanding than merely having no other gods before God. In fact, one could keep all the commandments and still not please God. Isaiah writes,

> The Lord says: "These people come near to Me with their mouth and honor Me with their lips, but their hearts are far from Me. Their worship of Me is made up only of rules taught by men. You obey My commandments, but your hearts are far from Me." (Isa. 29:13)

Again, I think of what parents want from their children. If children simply obey what their parents tell them, that is not, by itself, love.

It's following rules. The rules are important, but they don't define or replace love. How often have we seen children constricted by well-meaning rules that destroyed their spirits? That isn't love—either way.

Love for God's Commands. There seems to be an imbalance between the frequent statements of God's love for His people and the less frequent statements of man's love for God. Psalm 119 and others suggest a possible answer. Although the writer does not explicitly profess his love for God in the Psalm, there is a sense in which it's assumed. "I delight in Your commands.... I love Your commands... the earth is filled with your love.... Your unfailing love is my comfort.... Your law is my delight." All of these expressions imply that the writer loves God, but he never says it explicitly. God's love is the focus. The writer's love is a response.

Why this reluctance to speak of a person's love for God? Given my own contemplation of this it seems likely that it's the result of human awareness of the disparity between the magnitude of God's love for man and what man is capable of returning to God. As a child I didn't think about this. My love for God was not different in nature from my love for my parents, my siblings or others. Love was love. The adult *me* is very aware of the difference in my capacity to love as compared to God's capacity.

What I long for and search for are ways for my love to grow. I think the key to that begins with understanding—knowing the limitations of my love and yet believing it can be greater, wanting it to be greater. As in my childhood experience of asking God for wisdom I am in a sense asking Him for greater love for Him and for others. Just wanting to be more loving toward God and my neighbors will, I believe, cause my love to grow. Wanting is the first step toward having.

As I ponder Psalm 119 I am aware of the emphasis on God's statues, commands, precepts and His law. I note also the writer's acceptance of God's promised love: "May Your unfailing love be my comfort, according to Your promise to Your servant" (v. 76). The emphasis here is on loving God through following His commands. "Oh, how I love Your law!" (v. 97). There is more to this love than merely loving a set of rules. It is a love for words from, direction from, and promises from God. The love is not merely for the laws, but for the God Who blesses by giving words as direction.

There remains the reluctance...I don't know how else to understand it...the reluctance to speak of man's love for God. The closest the Psalmist comes is the request, "Turn to me and have mercy on me, as You always do to those who love Your name" (ver.132). Why not the direct statement, "to those who love You?" The writer can't bring himself to be so familiar with God.

God's Elevation of Human Love. As much as the absence of expressions of man's love for God in Scripture perplexes me I admire and share the reluctance to presume that the love of a human can be placed on the same scale as the love of God for humans. Only God can elevate human love to a level worthy of Him.

In a beautiful and extended description of the relationship between God and His people Moses interweaves several aspects of this relationship in Deuteronomy 7:5-13. In this passage Moses instructs the people to destroy the pagan symbols they find in the land, including everything that competes with God (ver. 5).

Let's see. What are our altars?—stages and stadiums, sacred stones—fine jewelry, Asherah poles—luxury cars, perhaps, and idols—too many to list. There is a time for people who love God to denounce and resist with all loving means the trivialization of things holy. It's so easy, in the name of attracting people to God, to engage in activities that do not honor God. I think He would say, "If you have to bribe them to get them to worship, I'd just as soon you not bother."

Why God Chose the Hebrews - BECAUSE. With anticipation we await the answer to the question of why God chose the Hebrews. "It was because the LORD loved you and kept the oath that He swore to your ancestors" (Deut. 7:7, 8). That's it? "Because?" I'm thrilled that when the answer is given as to why He chose the Hebrews God can't really explain, or chooses not to. If He chose to explain it, I'm not sure it would be love—it would be an equation.

That is for me a huge conundrum as I explore what it means to love God. In the unlikely case that I end up actually explaining it will it ruin everything? Yes, probably—if I could! I've come to realize that I can't quantify what it means to love God. A part of the mystique of loving God is that it demands of me my highest and best effort, yet my efforts always fall short.

But I am a man, and not God. What does it mean for a human to love God? I think mankind has toyed with that, exploited that, and used that to impose one group's will on another. I know that in the name of loving God religious groups have exonerated despicable behavior. I am attempting to understand my own nature and destiny through studying what it means to love God. After I write the last word I think it will come down to this—I don't know but I'm going to keep on trying.

I don't write that as resignation. I write it as celebration. Do I want to know why I love God and what that means? Of course. Do I expect to discover the ultimate answer? Yes, but not in this lifetime. So what? God is my partner in this quest. It's the quest not merely of humans. It is the quest also, I think, of God.

Love in the Promised Land - A Disappointment. After the initial coming to awareness of God's love as described in Genesis, there is nothing that rivals God's great act of love in delivering His people from Egypt. In fact, that event becomes the defining moment in God's relationship with the Jews, even to this day. The giving of the law is seen as a continuation of His love for His people, but the implementation of that loving covenant does not go smoothly. The history of Israel is a roller coaster of falling away and being restored.

The commandments provide the connecting link between every stage of Israel's history. They are given in the wilderness. They continue to shape all of life for the Israelites as they take possession of the Promised Land, and after they are settled there. The people constantly forget God, follow other gods. God's repeated punishment followed by forgiveness is itself a demonstration of His patient and enduring love. Israel forsakes God and His prophets call them back..."Return to Me." (Neh. 1:9; Is. 44:22; Jer. 4:1; Zech. 1:3; Mal. 3:7, *et al.*)

Love and Justice. It must be noted that the Old Testament makes a strong connection between love and justice. God ponders whether He should hide His intention to destroy Sodom from Abraham. He concludes, "No, for I have chosen him, that he may charge his children and his household after him to keep the way of the LORD by doing righteousness and justice; so that the LORD may bring about for Abraham what He has promised him" (Gen. 18:19).

God's promise to Abraham will result from Abraham's keeping "the way of the Lord." What does keeping the way of the Lord mean?—"doing righteousness and justice." From this we conclude that the heirs of God's promise to bless the nations will be those who do righteousness and justice. Righteousness and justice go together and are expressions of man's love for God.

Later in the wilderness Moses asks the people what God requires. He lists the requirements—" Only to fear the LORD your God, to walk in all His ways, to love Him, to serve the LORD your God with all your heart and with all your soul, and to keep the commandments..." (Deut 10:12-13). He tells the people that though all the heavens belong to God, "yet the Lord set his heart in love on your ancestors alone and chose you" (10:14,15). God is then described as one "Who executes justice for the orphan and the widow, and Who loves the strangers" (v. 18).

Justice is a frequent theme in the wisdom literature. God loves justice. It's one of His dominant characteristics. Justice and love are almost synonymous in places. The Psalmist sings of God's love and justice, showing his love by living a blameless life and promoting justice by silencing those who slander their neighbors (Ps. 101).

No less a person than the Queen of Sheba said to King Solomon, "Because your God loved Israel and would establish them forever, He has made you king over them, that you may execute justice and righteousness" (2 Chr. 9:8). How interesting that a foreign ruler would first recognize that making Solomon king was an expression of God's love for Israel followed by the observation that Solomon's role was to "execute justice and righteousness."

The prophets make justice and love central to their message. Micah repeats Moses' question, "What does the Lord require of you?" His answer is, "To act justly and to love mercy and to walk humbly with your God" (Mic. 6:7, 8). The prophets didn't initiate this emphasis on justice but it is a strong element in their message. It's not the sacrifice of thousands of rams or rivers of oil that pleases God. God requires justice and mercy.

Justice in the Old Testament doesn't refer so much to punishment of one's enemies as to showing mercy to them. Justice means taking care of orphans, widows and strangers. Justice is not served when the helpless are neglected and strangers treated with hostility. This isn't the "eye for an eye" justice that Jesus associated with the law. It's an acceptance of responsibility for those in distress, showing love just as God has shown love for His people. This is the background against which Jesus appears, albeit, some two hundred years after the last prophet called for justice.

XI.
The Pinnacle of Love – Jesus

Many books have been written on what Jesus taught about love. After as many more have been written there still won't be enough to do justice to the subject. I don't intend to add just one more, but to revisit a few statements Jesus made about loving God, and to try to understand His demands.

I've described my own journey as one who loves God and the demands that's made on me. I've described God's dealings with all of His creation from the beginning. Now let's look at how Jesus describes God's intent for man in the commandment to love God with all one's heart, soul, mind and strength. I'll shorten the commandment to "loving God with all your heart," but that includes "soul, mind and strength."

Surprising Love. The first thing Jesus says about love is a real surprise. It's not poetic. It's not a theological pronouncement. It certainly isn't a platitude. It's totally unexpected, and illogical. "Love your enemies." Abrupt. Unprecedented. Unreasonable. It's the very first statement Jesus makes about love as recorded in both Matthew and Luke (Matt. 5:44, Lk. 6:27). Jesus intends to get His followers' attention with that statement. He acknowledges what everyone already knows, that we naturally love our fellows. For Him that's not enough. He demands that we also love those who view us as enemies.

This sets the stage for the almost impossible demands that Jesus makes of those who think they might want to follow Him. It comes at the beginning of His attack on loveless religion in what we call the "Sermon on the Mount." Even a casual reading shows that this teacher sets a new ceiling on love. The old ceiling was "love your neighbor." The new ceiling is to love all the way up through loving your enemies. WOW!

The concept of loving God goes almost all the way back to the beginning of the Bible. But for the first time it's expanded to include the unthinkable. The very word "love" is redefined when it embraces even our enemies. It's a whole new concept in the teachings of Jesus. It's one concept to love your neighbor. It's a totally different thing to love your enemies. How is that even possible?

Sure, we use love in all kinds of ways. A mother's love—perhaps the most tender expression of love. Love for your spouse. Love for a friend. Love of country. Love of fishing or golfing. Loving chocolate cake. There are so many different levels of love. But to love my enemy? If we're paying attention, that stops us in our tracks—which is exactly what Jesus intends. This is a "knock-you-off-your-feet" love, and Jesus doesn't want there to be any mistaking it for any love known up until that demand.

He compares it to what religion has come to accept as love—the SHOW of loving God. That kind of love is seen in the hypocrisy that has been passed off as worship of God. He doesn't name names but simply uses as an example those who love to pray where they can be seen. They don't love praying. They love being seen by others. He calls them hypocrites (Matt. 6:1-18).

Above All Other Loves. Jesus then narrows the focus of the love He demands of His followers. Loving God means an all-possessing love that excludes all other loves. He compares this love to a slave who can have only one master. That kind of love demands that we be slaves to God (Matt. 6:24). Just to be sure the point isn't missed He adds, You can't serve God and wealth. That is admittedly extreme but it is what Jesus requires.

This is a heavy demand...but it gets tougher. If you love parents or children more than Jesus you aren't worthy of Him (Matt. 10:37). That's what He says. This acknowledges that the love a person has for parents and children is important and a very high level of love. Jesus demands a love that is measured by a gauge where He and His Kingdom are at the top, and parents and children are below that.

> Whoever comes to Me and does not hate father and mother, wife and children, brothers and sisters, yes, and even life itself, cannot be My disciple. Whoever does not carry the cross and follow Me cannot be My disciple. (Luke 14:26, 27)

This is obviously hyperbole as Jesus recognizes that healthy love includes love of self, as even the great commandment acknowledges. Yet there is the reality that to follow Christ means to "carry the cross." So great is Jesus' demand for total love that all else is hated by comparison.

By this stage of the boot camp training His followers must have been in shock. They had enlisted because of Jesus' irresistible call to devotion. He now removes all illusions that following Him will be a picnic. That's exactly what He intends.... It's what He still intends—to weed out the ones who want one foot in the Kingdom and the other in the world. We can't understand what Jesus means by loving God with all our heart until we accept the reality that it's almost impossibly difficult to love God as much as Jesus demands. Difficult? Yes, but it's the goal. Impossible? Maybe, but His followers must try.

Impossible Love. Let's take a look at this impossible love. One day a man comes to Jesus and asks what he must do to get eternal life. Jesus tells him, "Obey the commandments." He lists a few and adds the one that isn't among the ten—"Love your neighbor as yourself." The young man tells Jesus he's done all these things, but he still feels something is missing. Jesus tells him to sell all his possessions and give the money to the poor. Then he will have treasure in heaven. The man must have made a good impression because Jesus invites him to become one of His followers (Matt. 19:16-26).

Jesus didn't tell everyone to sell all of their possessions. In fact, the disciples apparently didn't sell their boats. After Jesus' crucifixion they returned to their fishing...and their boats. It wasn't standard practice to sell everything before a person could follow Christ. Peter did claim that he and the other apostles had left everything to follow Jesus, but that seemed not to have applied to their boats and nets (Matt. 19:27, Mk. 10:28).

It's evident that this man loves his possessions more than he loves God and more than he wants eternal life. It's as simple as that. He wants eternal life, but not THAT much. He goes away grieving because "he had many possessions." This causes Jesus to remark how hard it is for a rich person to enter the kingdom of heaven, harder than for a camel to go through the eye of a needle. To love God with all your heart means that God is more important than anything else, including your possessions.

The disciples hear Jesus loud and clear. His statement about the camel and the eye of the needle strikes home. "Then who can be saved?" they ask. Jesus responds, "For mortals it is impossible, but for God all things are possible" (Matt. 19:26, Mark 10:27).

I believe we can ask with equal incredulity, "Then who can truly love God with all her heart?" The answer is the same one Jesus gives His disciples. Only God can lead us to that level of love. I can't claim any credit for God being more important to me than possessions. It's not what I've done that has put the Kingdom of God within me. It's what God's done. I've said it before, and I repeat it—I don't know why I love God. I just do. I give God the credit for this because I believe He put it in my heart to want to love Him. But it's up to me to love Him with my whole heart.

Love in Turbulent Times. We live in turbulent times. Terrorist attacks produce fear. Economic ups and downs produce uncertainty. Natural disasters literally shake our world. I ask myself, what is my source of satisfaction and joy? Can I find joy in a turbulent world? Will I have enough for retirement? Is anyplace in the world safe? While these questions cause me some concern, they do not rob me of the desire to explore what it means to love God. If anything they cause me to realize that my love for God, family and friends is more important—and more enduring—than physical security, possessions or a certain future. In fact, my love for God is the one certainty.

That doesn't mean that safety, financial resources, and confidence that the world is firm beneath me aren't important to me. They are.

I like being able to travel and feel secure. I like not having to pinch every penny. I like living in a nice house. By most standards I'm a rich man—and so are most of the people who will read this. We live in the safest, richest, most secure country in the world. I love America above all other nations. Yet my American citizenship is not the most important thing to me. I am first of all a citizen of the Kingdom of God.

Neither fear, nor concern for possessions, nor anything else can be allowed to interfere with my love for God. In spite of humble beginnings I've always felt rich. Being rich in money has never been my aim in life. Having money and being rich are not one and the same for me. I can say along with Paul, "I know what it is to have little, and I know what it is to have plenty" (Phil. 4:12). If money had been important to me, I would have chosen a different vocation. I try to be rich in love.

I haven't come close to making the sacrifices Paul made to preach the gospel. I've preached the gospel most of my life, but I can't say it's caused me a lot of sacrifices, at least not of anything that's important to me. What I gave up was a life of pursuing nuclear physics, mathematics and astronomy. I turned away from what I enjoyed most—physics and science, in order to pursue what I loved most—God and His Kingdom. I still follow the advances in physics and astronomy and nuclear engineering because those areas fascinate me. I pursue my journey to the Kingdom because God and I love each other.

Is it hard to put the Kingdom first? Yes and no. It would be harder for me to pursue any other passion than God. I sing, "I love Thy Kingdom Lord, the house of Thine abode," and I think of how I can't even describe that Kingdom from a scientific point of view. Yet for me the Kingdom is intimately bound up in "the house of Thine abode" which I take to be both heaven and this physical world that God created for His, and my, pleasure and enjoyment.

Again, I can say along with the Apostle Paul, "But our citizenship is in heaven, and it is from there that we are expecting a Savior, the Lord Jesus Christ" (Phil. 3:20). Whatever I passed up in not following the path of exploring this marvelous universe through the eyes of physics will be more than made up when I see my Savior face to face. As Paul writes, "For now we see in a mirror, dimly, but then we will see face to face. Now I know only in part; then I will know fully, even as I have been fully known" (1 Cor. 13:12). I most want to know Christ and the power of His resurrection (Phil. 3:10).

The Greatest Commandment. Matthew writes of an instance in which a group of Pharisees approach Jesus. One of them puts Jesus to the test asking, "Which is the greatest commandment?" Jesus tells him that the greatest commandment is:

> You shall love the Lord your God with all your heart, and with all your soul, and with all your mind." This is the greatest and first commandment. And a second is like it: "You shall love your neighbor as yourself." On these two commandments hang all the law and the prophets. (Matt. 22:37-40)

Matthew does not tell us how the Pharisees respond to this seemingly provocative statement of Jesus—that all of the law and prophets hang on these two commandments. Jesus avoids the lawyer's test by giving him an answer that was not easy to argue with.

Jesus then turns the questioning on the Pharisees asking, "What do you think of the Messiah?" (Matt. 22:42). No one dares to answer

Him. They aren't looking for answers. They're looking to test Him to the point of failure. In doing so they expose their own failure to be truly devoted to God, probably without even realizing they are doing so.

In Mark's reporting of this incident he adds some interesting details not given by Matthew or Luke. Mark writes that the man replies to Jesus that loving God and neighbor is "much more important than all whole burnt offerings and sacrifices." In response Jesus says to him, "You are not far from the Kingdom of God" (Mk. 12:28-34).

The man's reply places love for God and neighbor on a higher level than religious acts such as burnt offerings and sacrifices. Jesus validates the man's realization by saying, "you are not far from the Kingdom of God." Even then, the implication is "not far, but still not quite close enough."

Jesus doesn't say that the religious rituals are unimportant. He says that loving God and neighbor is more important than all the religious ceremonies. Nothing in the world is to interfere with or compete for our love for God. It's a high demand. Just as importantly, nothing is to keep us from acting on that love.

The Good Samaritan. Luke's Gospel alone reports that the lawyer still wants to justify himself and asks Jesus yet another question. "And who is my neighbor?" In answer Jesus tells him one of the most famous and intriguing of the parables.

A man left beaten and half dead is passed by a priest and a Levite, two men who should see him as a brother. A Samaritan, who would under ordinary circumstances be seen by the beaten man as an outcast, even an enemy, stops and takes care of him. Jesus asks the expert in the law which was neighbor to the beaten man? The expert replies, maybe with some reluctance, "The one who had mercy on him." Jesus tells him, "Go and do likewise" (Lk. 10:25-37).

The expert had asked one of the right questions—'"Who is my neighbor?" Jesus' vivid illustration allows the man to answer his own question. The spirit within him overcomes his prejudice against Samaritans and allows him to acknowledge that *any* other person in need is his neighbor, even his enemies. It's revealing that the man doesn't respond, "The Samaritan." He scorns the Samaritans. He isn't quite ready for that leap. Jesus confronts him with the reality that until he loves God more than his own prejudices he will not inherit eternal life.

It doesn't end there for me. I want the expert to ask the next question, "How do I love God that much—with all my heart?" This question is implicit in the example that loving God means loving even our enemies. The example of the Samaritan becomes a gauge of what it means to love God. It's one of the most important measures. The text puts us to the test. Do we love God more than we hate our enemies? It's a test that, sadly, in my experience, many Christians do not pass.

Christians have been sorely tested by the hateful behavior of Muslim terrorists who in the name of God have carried out terrible atrocities against those of us whom they see as enemies. In response I have heard responses from Christian people who propose that we should retaliate with punishing, destructive attacks that destroy even innocent Muslims. My response is to ask, "How is this different from the "eye for an eye" teaching of the law?"

I don't claim to have an easy answer for the violent and hateful actions of terrorists who in the name of God attack us. I do believe that if we truly follow Jesus we must be careful not to respond with vengeful and hateful actions. I am all for protecting the safety and well-being of the citizens of our country. I can even accept that it might be necessary to destroy the capability of our enemies to inflict damage on us. What I cannot accept is allowing our enemies to cause us to act out of hatred and vengeance. That would be antithetical to our devotion to loving God. I believe our love for God is being put to the test in how we respond to our enemies.

The Gold Standard. Jesus' teaching about loving God and loving our neighbor and enemies is difficult for us to fathom—beyond our comprehension, really. It is what He finally does in response to His own love for God that demonstrates to us, and at the same time confronts us with, the ultimate test. He had told His disciples, "No one has greater love than this, to lay down one's life for one's friends" (Jn. 15:13). He completes His mission by dying on the cross out of love for God and all humankind.

It is one thing for Jesus to say, "Sell all that you have and give it to the poor, leave your fishing, your job, everything, and follow me." This laying down one's life for one's friends is asking for a willingness to die, if necessary, in the service of God. It means loving God more than one loves her own life. What does one say after that statement?

Jesus' mission was very clear to Him. He knew that it would be fulfilled with His sacrifice on the cross. Just so we don't miss how terribly difficult the demand is, even He questions it. In the garden agony He pleads, "My Father, if it is possible, let this cup pass from Me; yet not what I want but what You want" (Matt. 26:39). It is no easy thing, this loving God more than loving one's own life. The love is put to the test in the decision to do, not what He wants, but what God wants.

Most of us will never face that ultimate test, and seeking it would be wrong. I don't need to go looking for some way to die in order to love God with all my heart. Doesn't spending one's life in the selfless service of others amount to the same sacrifice? Ah, yes and no. There is something so compelling about the thought of denying oneself, so to speak, and taking up one's cross in some dramatic gesture of self-sacrifice. It's probably equally difficult to simply be kind and loving to every person we meet, turning the other cheek, walking the extra mile, and giving to him who asks. Try it some time and I think you'll discover it's very difficult to put another person first EVERY time. I can do it pretty well when I really put my mind to it but it's so easy to become distracted by my own needs and wants. Loving God calls to us to do even the smallest kindness as well as being willing to make the greatest sacrifice.

Returning to the Mountain. I write these words on a Good Friday afternoon as I look forward to revisiting Jesus' supreme act of love in dying on the cross. Why do I return to this act of remembrance year after year? Is it that I hope one day to get it just right, to fully internalize Jesus' supreme sacrifice? Or is it that I don't yet fully understand its meaning and significance and feel that I can do so only through endless repetition? No, it's that I've pretty much made it a part of my experience and have probed its depths of devotion. I return to it as a beloved place that brings not so much any new insights as celebration of the old insights.

There are mountaintops to which I return, not so much to see something new but to feel something of myself of which I'm aware only when standing on their lofty heights. There are paintings that I gaze at again and again, not because I see anything new in them so much as that they cause me to experience something of myself and the world that happens only in their presence. I love being with family and friends, not so much because of discovery of anything new but for the realization of that essential part of me which is missing when they are not present.

I want to love God to the degree that Jesus did. How do I go about moving toward that lofty goal? I move a bit closer each time I open my own heart to His incredible sacrifice. In remembering His sacrifice I experience a renewed desire to love God as fully as it's possible for a human being to do so.

I will never climb Mt. Everest, at least not to the top. It's beyond my capabilities at this time in my life. About a dozen years ago I did climb Mt. Whitney—all the way to the top, up and down in one day! It was one of my life's goals, and a realistic one in my fifties. I now delight in the accomplishment of others who summit Mt. Everest. I'm glad they do it, for a part of my spirit climbs along with them.

In the same way, I don't expect in this lifetime to love God with the perfection I see in Jesus. I want to, and I'm trying, but I'm not perfect and any sin demonstrates I've fallen short of the mark. Along with Paul I must confess that I fall short. Paul concludes, "Wretched man that I am! Who will rescue me from this body of death? Thanks be to God through Jesus Christ our Lord!" (Rom. 7:24, 25). I'm glad Jesus reached that summit because He took with Him a part of my spirit. In my own way I was, and am, with Him.

In this life I'm weighed down by too many human frailties. I'm not talking about age or illness but rather the human condition.

I can say that I hate no one, but I occasionally treat some people less than kindly. I can say that I believe God will continue to provide for the necessities of my life as He does for the birds and flowers, but I occasionally have some anxiety. So, how can I say with any conviction that I want to reach the pinnacle of loving God with all my heart?

This is precisely where that summit of love saves me from myself. In the very moment that I realize I am slipping down the slope of loving self more than God, the commandment to love reaches out and grasps my hand, pulling me back from the abyss of selfishness and sinful pride. I have made a commitment to love God with all my heart. Confessing my failings allows the gift of Christ to atone for what I am lacking.

With that in mind I turn my imperfect eye toward the Perfect One Who got it right, Who achieved the pinnacle of love.

Jesus answered the question of what it means to love God with all one's heart with His supreme act of love. Jesus Himself set the standard when He willingly gave up His life. There it is. Would any doubt that a person who is willing to die for another, or for God, loves that other or God with all their heart? It's the gold standard of love.

Even a scoundrel who finds it in himself to die in place of another is judged to be a person of ultimate love. The words of the character Sydney Carton, in *A Tale of Two Cities,* comes to mind. Having lived a mostly wasted life Carton takes the place of the protagonist and substitutes himself as the victim of the guillotine. Just before he dies he utters bitter-sweet words of repentance and love, "It is a far, far better thing that I do, than I have ever done; it is a far, far better rest that I go to than I have ever known."

XII.
Love and the Commandments

How is it possible for a human being to love an invisible God? The search for an answer is a thread running through the entire Bible. Adam and Eve hear the sound of God walking in the Garden, and God speaks to them, but there is no indication that they see God. God speaks to Noah, Abraham and others but still does not appear. An angel appears to Moses "in a flame of fire out of a bush" and when Moses turns aside to look, God speaks to him out of the bush. While it's pretty clear that Moses doesn't actually see God, God instructs him to tell the elders, that He has appeared to him. So far as we know Moses saw only the bush and its flame.

There are other visual manifestations of God, most notably the pillar of cloud and fire. Hagar, Jacob, and Manoah declared they had seen God but in each case the text is clear that what they had seen was an angel of the Lord. In his Gospel, John declares that "No one has ever seen God" (1:18). He then proceeds to explain how God has now appeared to humankind in Jesus His Son.

I have stated that in order to love God, He must be real to us. I've dealt at length with the problem of how we can love without seeing. This is one of the great enigmas of our quest to love God. How can we really love a being we can't see? His essential obscurity is a huge detriment to our developing love for Him according to our usual understanding of love.

The writer of the Gospel of John shows a high interest both in the concept of how we love God as well as the answer to humankind's desire to see God. He alone notes Jesus' response to Thomas: "Have you believed because you have seen me? Blessed are those who have not seen and yet have come to believe" (Jn. 20:29).

Again in his first Epistle John writes, "No one has ever seen God; if we love one another, God lives in us..." (1 Jn. 4:12). The implication is that Christians see God in one another because "God lives in us." If we have any hope of loving God from a human point of view, we'll have to settle for directing that love toward our brothers and sisters. If we can't love them, whom we are able to see, we won't have a chance of loving God Whom we have not seen (I Jn. 4:19-20). Yet in his Gospel John goes to great lengths to persuade his readers that those who saw Jesus believed it was the same as seeing God. This connection between seeing God and seeing Jesus is interwoven with God's love in sending Jesus, His Son.

Love in the Gospel of John. John's first mention of love is in the familiar verse which every child learns in Sunday School. "For God so loved the world that He gave His only Son, so that everyone who believes in Him may not perish but may have eternal life" (Jn. 3:16). The emphasis here is what we've seen throughout the Bible—God's love for the world.

At first it seems that John is going to follow that familiar theme—God's overwhelming love for humankind. He does, but in a unique and unexpected way. He turns his attention immediately to Jesus' role in communicating and embodying God's love. His next reference to love is in a statement made by John the Baptist. The Baptist, in instructing his disciples, says, "The Father loves the Son and has placed all things in His hands. Whoever believes in the Son has eternal life; whoever disobeys the Son will not see life, but must endure God's wrath" (Jn. 3:35, 36).

Love the Father—Love the Son. John connects God's love for man very specifically to Jesus. John portrays Jesus in the exact role of the son in the parable of the wicked vine keepers. He doesn't repeat the parable that occurs in all three Synoptic Gospels but his entire Gospel is in a way a recounting of what actually happens between the Son and the tenants to whom He is sent (Matt. 21:38ff; Mk. 12:7ff; Lk. 20:9ff).

John omits the parable possibly because he wants to avoid its conclusion—the anger of the father and his punishing of the tenants with a "miserable death." This does not fit his purpose of portraying Jesus as the willing sacrificial gift sent by the loving Father. The Father reasons that those who have rejected His servant messengers will accept His Son. John just wants a different ending from that given in the parable. He wants the evil tenants to be persuaded by the patience and long-suffering of the Father. His whole Gospel reflects the desired conclusion of the tenants accepting the Son.

In the parable the tenants recognize the son for who he is, and kill him, thinking that if they kill the heir to the vineyard, they will inherit the property. In contrast, in John's Gospel the arrival of the Son, Jesus, leads to an argument of identity. Is He really the Son of the Father? On what does He base that claim? "Give us the proof," His Jewish opponents demand. They don't kill Him right off as in the parable. They simply reject His claim of being sent by the Father and are determined to kill Him because He was "calling God His own Father, thereby making Himself equal to God" (5:18).

John doesn't ignore the wickedness of those who reject Jesus. As already noted, his second use of the word "love" is, "People loved darkness rather than light because their deeds were evil" (3:19. He recognizes that the tenants are wicked, but he wants them to accept the Son, though in the end they do not.

I relate to John's approach perhaps in part because in my early understanding of God, while I was sorry for those who rejected Jesus, I believed that in the end they got what they deserved. It was so clear and simple. I was just a brash youth who didn't have to deal with the real world of people who wanted simple, and easy, answers on how to get along with God. The "simple" I understood—My way, my understanding. "Easy" on the other hand, just doesn't happen with God.

John knew the hearts of these Jewish opponents. They were devoted to God—at least to their understanding of God. They had poured their lives into keeping the law, maintaining the worship of God, and keeping the rituals pure and central to religious life. They had succeeded, at least for themselves, and now they were being challenged. That is never easy, as I can attest. It's painful to give up the legalistic system of one's own mind and heart in following God. Even those who start out wanting to be "pure in heart" can easily end up in a narrow rut that doesn't allow enough breadth to admit the love of God.

But John is unrelenting. He wants the narrow, "stiff-necked" opponents of Jesus to open their minds and hearts. Writing many years after the Jewish people have given clear signs of having missed the point John wants to give it one more try. "God sent His Son—it's so clear, just look at it again, and accept it."

I have been unrelenting in my own mission to present the love of God as I understand it through the teachings of Jesus. I've had to recognize that the rejection of Jesus in our world, both by unbelievers and believers in other religions, is so deeply entrenched that any hint of my failure to recognize the authenticity of their devotion to God can slam the door against any sense of brotherhood. My understanding of Jesus is that while He had the judgment to know who His enemies were, He has not made me judge in His place. I am to embody His love.

When Jesus confronts a group of His enemies among the Jews He accuses, "If God were your Father, you would love Me, for I came from God and now I am here. I did not come on My own, but He sent Me" (8:42). He denounces their failure to accept His claim to being God's Son and continues, "You are from your father the devil, and you choose to do your father's desires.... Whoever is from God hears the words of God. The reason you do not hear them is that you are not from God" (8:44-47).

Jesus is making a demand that no human had made before. Not only does He say that His Father has sent him, but He demands to be accepted as the Son of God Who has the authority to speak on behalf of His father, to forgive sins and to make Himself the judge of whether others are doing the will of His Father.

He goes a step further. At least a dozen times in John's Gospel Jesus equates "loving Me" with loving God. This is a new concept only hinted at in the other Gospels. It's central to John's understanding that man can now love God without the barrier of God's invisibility. In Jesus there is a new reality between God and man. For the first time in history humankind experiences the physical, visible, living presence of God. Jesus says to Philip, "Whoever has seen Me has seen the Father" (14:9). This is the revelation for which humans have been waiting.

From this point on John presents the teachings of Jesus with the assumption that when Jesus asks the disciples to love Him, He is asking them to love God. Equally, when He speaks of His love for the disciples He is saying it's the same as God loving them. While there are other nuances involved, the significant point is that loving God and loving Jesus are understood as being synonymous.

Loving One Another Equated with Loving Jesus. Jesus announces to His disciples that He is giving them a new commandment. With high expectations they await the revelation. Here it is. "Just as I have loved you, you also should love one another" (13:34). On the surface this seems a rather mild statement. It's not even close to being mild! This commandment puts their love for one another on the same level as His love for them. That means that their love for each other is equated with God's love for them. Their love is God's love! This idea is more fully developed in John's first Epistle, but is clearly implicit in this statement, and in later statements regarding the commandments.

How are the disciples to demonstrate their love for Jesus? By keeping "My commandments" (14:15, 21, 23; 15:9, 12, 17). These strong and repeated statements about keeping "My commandments" are easily assumed to be "The Commandments." On the surface this appears to be a reaffirmation of what Moses delivered, but without the tablets of stone. Our natural reaction is to ask for the list of commandments. Jesus doesn't provide it. There is no list. There are the words and the life of Jesus. These can't be expressed in a list of commandments alone.

Humans May Become Children of God. God's relationship with Jesus as His Son extends beyond Jesus. This relationship is also offered to all humans! John writes at the beginning of his Gospel, "But to all who received Him, who believed in His name, He gave power to become children of God, who were born, not of blood or of the will of the flesh or of the will of man, but of God" (1:12, 13). Coming as it does at the very beginning of the Gospel this statement takes on added significance in light of John's development of the relationship between loving Jesus and loving God. By receiving the Son we become daughters and sons of God.

John does not dwell on the concept of the followers of Jesus becoming the children of God, either in his Gospel or in his Epistles. It raises interesting, even intriguing, concepts which offer much food for thought. We must be content with the concept that when we love Jesus it is the same as loving God.

There is much more that we would like to know about this relationship we have with God through Jesus. Jesus does not claim that He has taught His disciples all they need to know about God's love, or for that matter, this new relationship of becoming children of God. The Holy Spirit will yet play a role—two roles, really. First, the Spirit will remind His followers of what Jesus has said. Second, it will "teach you everything" (14:26). Jesus promises that the Holy Spirit will continue to teach His followers what they need in the years ahead. This is a major paradigm shift from the tablets of stone. The tablets are an anchor with the past, which serves to provide stability. The commands of Jesus are dynamic and living, incapable of being codified in a list. The Pharisees had already attempted to do that, and Jesus has denounced them for it. Jesus' commands are to be written on people's hearts (Rom. 2:15; 2 Cor. 3:2, 3).

The Test. Many years ago I found myself sitting across the desk from an elder in the Church where I was the minister of education. I knew from previous conversations with him that he had an excellent knowledge of the Bible. My years of seminary education had given me only a slight edge in knowledge of Scripture, an edge which he enjoyed putting to the test.

He came quickly to the point. Pushing a type-written page across the desk, his grim face told me I was in for a challenge. I was young and inexperienced, in my first full-time ministry position. He was seasoned and had years of practice in intimidating young ministers. "I've prepared this test on the Bible," he announced. "I want you to give it to everyone who is teaching our Bible school classes."

"Oh brother," I thought. "It's already difficult to recruit enough teachers to have a fully staffed Bible school. This will drive half of them away even if we tell them it's just a study to help them teach better." I looked at the questions:

– Do you believe that Jesus was born of a virgin?
– Do you believe in the miracles?
– Do you believe the Bible is the inspired Word of God?

There was a whole page, single spaced.

The questions were not so difficult. They were just...numerous. There must have been fifty questions. I couldn't say "No" to the test without raising suspicion that I myself was soft on the basics of the faith. If I agreed to give it, my job of recruiting teachers would become much more difficult—and I felt no useful purpose would be served.

I read on through the list, not so much to see every question, but to give myself time to think. As I finished the questions it dawned on me .... The problem I was having with the list wasn't the questions that were on it. It was the questions that weren't on it that made it so impossible to accept.

I laid the page on the desk and pushed it back to him. "The problem with this test is that it doesn't ask the right questions," I explained. "What questions?" he shot back. "For starters, the two most important questions aren't on your test. The first is, 'Do you love the Lord your God with all your heart, soul, mind and strength?' The second is, 'Do you love your neighbor as yourself?'"

"Let's add them," he countered! "I can't do that," I replied. "If I don't see the answer to those questions in the lives of the people who are teaching our classes, it doesn't matter if they can answer all the others correctly. If one of them were to teach something contrary to the Bible, I would learn of it. It takes longer to see if they really love God and their neighbor. I don't know of any test that can figure that out ahead of time."

We had an interesting and helpful conversation. The man became my friend. In reality, I do think we should ask questions of those who teach children—but what questions? The basics of our faith are important, to be sure. The fact is, I've known a good number of people through the years who could correctly answer all the questions on that man's test, yet probably fail the missing questions about loving God and neighbor.

Our love for God is put to the test every day, both in our awareness of God and in our relationships and interactions with other people. Just as in marriage, it isn't simply saying "I do," and then we're done with it. It's an on-going, growing, demanding commitment that is never finished.

Jesus' Test of Love—Feed My Sheep. In a poignant moment following the resurrection, Jesus reminds Peter of the complexity of love. The disciples have abandoned their mission and returned to their fishing. How could they do that after all they had experienced in their three years with Him. How easily we profess our love for God in the victorious moments of life. How easily we abandon that love and revert to our pre-occupation with the concerns of this world when our plans fall apart. How faithfully our Lord recalls us to His mission. So, early the next morning Jesus, unexpected and unrecognized at first, prepares breakfast for His disciples on the shore of the Sea of Tiberius (Jn. 21:1-19). Calling to the disciples He suggests that they cast their nets on the other side of their boat. When that results in a large catch of fish, they realize that it's the Lord.

After they come ashore He serves them bread and fish. Peter is, no doubt, continuing to feel guilty for having denied Jesus three times, after asserting that even if everyone else deserted the Master he would not. Sitting there eating breakfast, Jesus asks Peter three times if he loves Him. Three times Peter affirms that he does.

Setting aside all the nuances embedded in Jesus' three repetitions of the question there is one overriding point. It doesn't matter how many times a person says he loves God. Saying it isn't the important thing. Showing it by one's actions is the only certain evidence of love. Three times Jesus responds to Peter's affirmation of love with the words, "Feed My sheep." Peter understands. "If you love me, don't just go back to fishing. If you love me, don't just make rash promises. That's not what counts. If you love me, take over my mission. What does it mean to love me? It means to spend your life taking care of my sheep. It means spending your life taking up my mission."

The mission of every follower of Jesus is to feed the Lord's sheep. Teachers, nurses, doctors, secretaries, business people, mothers, fathers and persons of every other occupation, or none, are offered boundless opportunities to feed the sheep of our Lord.

Awaiting the Teaching of the Spirit. Even all these events and teachings admittedly leave some loose ends, to which John seems to respond in his Epistles. We, along with John, await the teaching of the Spirit to lead us into a fuller and more complete understanding. Each of the writings of the New Testament touches on this subject of loving God. As John writes, we could fill the world with books on the subject and still not cover all that Jesus did (Jn. 21:25). We must allow the Spirit to continue to teach us through our own experience.

As already noted, Jesus demonstrates the ultimate expression of loving God in accepting His mission to die on the cross as a sacrifice for the sins of humankind. This message of sacrifice of self for others is a recurring theme in the writings of Paul and other books of the New Testament. I will not deal with each passage, but pause only to note that Paul acknowledges that all the commandments are summed up in this, "Love your neighbor as yourself" (Rom. 13:9).

In what is known as the "Love Chapter" of the Bible Paul describes the many facets of what it means to love, and perhaps most profoundly acknowledges that it can't be put into words (1 Cor. 13).

Any attempt to make a list ends up showing us how far short such a list falls.

John's Epistles—Living in the Light. After years of reflection John has additional thoughts he wishes to add to what he said about loving God in his Gospel. He hasn't changed his views, but he knows there's more to be said. He himself is also still being led by the Spirit into "all the truth" (Jn. 16:13). His emphasis on Jesus' teaching to "keep my commandments" had perhaps caused Christians to revert to a new legalism. That's what "The Test" offered by my friend represented. It's so easy to want to simplify our love for God to a list. I believe that one of the major purposes of John's Epistles is to address the impression that loving God means keeping THE commandments, whatever form they take.

In his three Epistles, John confronts head-on the question of what it means to love God. In his first Epistle the word "love" occurs over forty times. Obviously the subject of love continues to weigh heavily on John's mind, as it does on mine.

It's very difficult to organize the thoughts of the first Epistle. It's as though John is following a complicated thread of reasoning that doesn't lend itself to clear organization. The certainty of knowing where a person stands with Jesus is very important to him. The word "know" occurs thirty-two times, all in connection with the reader's having assurance that they know Jesus and are among the children of God. One such defining passage states:

> Now by this we may be **sure** that we know him, if we **obey His commandments**. Whoever says, "I have come to know Him," but does not **obey His commandments**, is a liar,

and in such a person the truth does not exist; but whoever **obeys His word**, truly in this person the love of God has reached perfection. By this we may be **sure** that we are in Him (1 Jn. 2:3-5). (all emphasis mine)

Distinctive in this passage is the repetition of the word "sure." John wishes to provide assurance to his readers that they "know Him," that is, Jesus. He states it twice. What is it that gives that assurance? Twice again he answers, "obey His commandments." As if to reinforce this assurance he states it yet another way, "obeys His word." I believe John is making a clear distinction between Jesus' commandments and the commandments in the law.

The Old Commandment in a New Light. I see this as the heart of John's First Epistle. Now we must ask again, what exactly are "his commandments?" First of all, it seems certain that the old commandment where it had been heard before (2:7) was in Leviticus where it is written, "love your neighbor as yourself" (Lev. 19:18). Significantly, this is extended to include aliens living among them. "The alien living with you must be treated as one of your native-born. Love him as yourself, for you were aliens in Egypt" (Lev. 19:34). This is important because in other passages the first Epistle indicates this love is specifically for "their brothers and sisters" (3:11, 4:21). We are reminded of the lawyer's question to Jesus, "Who is my neighbor?" (Lk. 10:25-37).

It's interesting to note that John states, "I am writing you no new commandment, but an old commandment" (2:7). In the very next verse he states, "Yet I am writing you a new commandment that is true in Him and in you, because the darkness is passing away and the true light is already shining.... Whoever loves a brother or sister lives in the light..." (2:8-10).

These seemingly contradictory statements give us a valuable insight into John's thought process. On the one hand the old commandments remain, yet they are seen in the light of the new reality which Jesus has brought. It's a merging of the truth of the old darkness that "is passing away and the true light <that> is already shining" (2:8). An awareness of this juxtaposition of the old with the new is necessary to understanding John's thought.

We return to our question of, "what are these new commandments?" It is not totally clear what the "new commandments" are or what "his commandments" are. There is a moment of focus where John states:

And this is His commandment, that we should believe in the name of His Son Jesus Christ and love one another, just as He has commanded us. (1 Jn. 3:23)

We don't need to sort out all the other statements Jesus makes about loving our brothers or obeying His commandments. This is a crystal clear statement as to what is meant by His commandments. His commandments are that we should believe in the name of God's Son Jesus Christ and love one another. Notice that I've also repeated it, as did John, just to be sure it's clear! It's so easy to miss its clear simplicity.

John also makes it clear what it means to love God:

We love because He first loved us. If anyone says, "I love God," yet hates his brother, he is a liar. For anyone who does not love his brother, whom he has seen, cannot love God, Whom he has not seen. And He has given us this command: Whoever loves God must also love his brother (1 Jn. 4:19-21).

Love between man and God originates with God, Who first loved us. John then clearly addresses the necessity of our loving God, and what that means—one loves God by loving his brother.

This clear statement of how we love God is repeated in John's second Epistle. Here it is also identified as the old, yet new commandment:

> But now, dear lady, I ask you, not as though I were writing you a new commandment, but one we have had from the beginning, **let us love one another**. (my emphasis) And this is love, that we walk according to His commandments; this is the commandment just as you have heard it from the beginning—you must walk in it (2 Jn. 5, 6).

The "new commandment" clearly is, "let us love one another." He finds it necessary to repeat, "this is the commandment." The attention given to this matter indicates the importance John attached to his readers' understanding what he meant by "commandments." He repeats the word "commandment(s)" three times in these two verses. He didn't want the new commandment to be interpreted as little more than the law with a heavy dose of love.

Obedience vs. Love. I feel the **tension** between obedience and love. We probably all do. The commandments are important—essential and fundamental, but Jesus changes what is at the heart of the commandments. In the Old Testament the foundation of the commandments was obedience—just DO it. In Jesus' teaching the heart, the center, of His commandments is love—do it because you LOVE Jesus.

As a child, loving God for me consisted of keeping His commandments—Yes, the Ten. The only thing that has changed in the intervening years between child and sexagenarian (don't bother to look it up—someone in their sixties) is the diminished number of Jesus' commandments. As a child, the commandments were too numerous to count. As a follower of Christ the number has reduced itself to two, though both are filled with myriads of dimensions— "Love Me, and love one another."

Written on a mental tablet of stone, these commandments were reborn in me in a most unlikely place. It happened in the most desolate island one can possibly imagine—the island country of Haiti. There, surrounded by a sea of poverty, I heard no voice, saw no vision, and encountered no burning bush except the unquenchable fire of the human spirit.

It was in Haiti on May 1, 2009, that an epiphany lighted my heart. I had accompanied a medical team which provides a biannual clinic at the Northwest Haiti Christian Mission. My assignment was to teach a class in the Mission's Bible College. The class was for Haitian students who were preparing to be ministers. The title of the course was, "What Does It Mean to Love God?"

There were some forty students in the class, many of whom had traveled for hours on foot to attend the class. Since I don't speak Creole an interpreter provided communication between the students and me. It didn't take an interpreter to make me aware of their totally different perspective on God and life. While they were without exception materially impoverished, they had a vibrant spirit that reinvigorated my own. I loved being among them. Their excitement about God was contagious.

All of life for them revolved around one thing—having enough food to survive. Yet they had walked, some of them for many miles, to be in a class where they could study the Bible. Their thin bodies hungered for the Word of God and for understanding of how they could bring spiritual nourishment to their fellow Haitians.

As we dealt with the Scriptures about God loving us and us loving God, I found it very difficult to fall back on my usual stories and examples. Most of my stories just didn't connect with the simple lives of these dynamic people. My experiences, I realized, were set in a place of wealth and plenty and anxiety for things which were meaningless to them.

These Haitian students were eager and full of enthusiasm. They were eager to learn more about the love of God. They hungered as much for God as they did for physical food. Their worship was spirited and optimistic, filled with the urgency of vibrant spirits determined to dance on dirt. From them I realized that the key to loving God was present in my first thoughts as a child.

What Commandments? I asked the students if they loved God. There was a chorus of responses—*"Oui, oui!"* I then asked, "What does that mean, to love God?" "To obey him," said several through the interpreter. "To keep His commandments," others added. "What commandments?" I prodded. There was a general outburst as everyone joined in. "What are they saying?" I asked the interpreter. He smiled as he tried to keep up with their lively responses. "Don't kill. Don't steal. Don't commit adultery. Don't lie. Don't take the name of God in vain." I didn't even try to list them all. One thing was clear. Loving God was about following His rules.

We spent time studying the passages of Scripture that explore God's love for man—His enduring love, His steadfast love, and His long-suffering love. In the last class I focused on Jesus' response to the lawyer who asked, "Which commandment in the law is the greatest?" Jesus answers, "You shall love the Lord your God with all your heart, and with all your soul, and with all your mind. This is the greatest and first commandment. And a second is like it: You shall love your neighbor as yourself" (Matt. 22:34-39).

I have looked at this passage many times through the years, but on this occasion the words which followed glowed with new light on these two commands. Jesus concludes, "On these two commandments hang all the law and the prophets" (Matt. 22:40). In my mind connections slammed together and finally made sense of the passage in John's Gospel, "If you love Me, you will keep My commandments" (Jn. 14:15).

I asked the class again which commandments Jesus was talking about. They repeated as before, "No other Gods, don't kill, don't commit adultery." I pointed to the wording of Jesus' statement—"My commandments." "What are Jesus' commandments?" I repeated. Once again there was a buzz through the class as many began to speak at once. "What are they saying?" I asked the interpreter. "They're saying, 'Love God and love one another!'"

That's it. Keep Jesus' commands. What are His commands? Just two: Love God. Love one another. There are other fundamental beliefs, of course, but all of them rest on these two.

This question of what it means to love God really is all about keeping His commandments. That is the surprising answer to which I have been irresistibly led. "If you love Me, you will keep My commandments." Through all the years of searching it was there in my first thoughts as a child—but not as I could understand it then. Jesus was not talking about a list of rules and obedience. He was talking about the heart and love.

No bride in her right mind would say, "If you love me you'll follow all these rules and conditions." What both bride and groom commit to is to love and to cherish for life. Then they go about figuring out what that means.

So it is with God. We commit to love Him with all our heart, soul, mind and strength. The joy and excitement of life consists in figuring out what that means.

Is That Really All? Is it really possible that it all comes down to this...that loving God is totally a matter of how we treat other people? Again and again that is where Scripture and my own heart lead me. Is it true that I will finally be judged not by getting theology just right, not by religious observances, and not by my words about God? Is showing love to other people at the heart of what loving God is all about? Yes, loving others is at the heart of loving God, but it's not the totality of loving God. There is more.

Conclusion
The Father's Business

Not By Bread Alone. Jesus said, quoting from Deuteronomy, "It is written, 'One does not live by bread alone, but by every word that comes from the mouth of God'" (Matt. 4:4; Deut. 8:3). Loving God isn't solely about feeding the hungry, visiting the sick, and taking care of the poor. Jesus did more than that. Even at the age of twelve He wandered off to talk to the teachers in the temple. When chastised for it He explained that He was doing His Father's business. What is God's business for us? Scripture and our own experience give some examples.

Living a Full Life with Others. Jesus' first miracle was turning water into wine, arguably giving a drink to someone who was thirsty, but hardly fitting the criteria of "the least of these" mentioned in the last judgment. He fasted in the desert, went off alone on occasion to pray, dined with tax collectors and friends, and even walked on water—which could be seen as indulging in a bit of personal enjoyment. In short, one of the ways He showed His love for God was by loving life to the fullest.

Truth, Trust, Teaching. In Paul's great reflection on love he acknowledges that even if he gives all he possesses to the poor, but lacks love, he gains nothing (1 Cor. 13). It's even more complex than that. Jesus' depiction of the judgment scene and the indictment, "I was hungry and you did not feed me," may be the bottom line, but it isn't the whole page of love. Love according to Paul includes discovering truth, providing protection, trusting, hoping, and not giving up. Immediately after the great chapter on love he observes that his readers are to "pursue love," but that they should especially prophesy in order to build up, encourage and console the church (I Cor. 14:1-4).

Using Our Gifts. On a more practical level I think of what I cherish most in those I love. My wife shows love by a multitude of things she does for me, for our children, and for others. I love her not just for the things she does for me. I love the gift of music that she possesses—a blessing to me and many others. Her music is one of the ways she loves God. If she were to ignore that talent, that is, not develop and use it, would she not be guilty of what another parable condemns in the man who buried his talent in the ground? He was sent packing into eternal darkness for being a poor steward.

Art as Loving God. I think of Van Gogh again. What if, instead of being fanatical about his painting on canvas, he had spent his time visiting those in prison and painting, not pictures, but the houses of poor people? Would humanity be better or worse off if he had neglected painting his masterpieces? I believe that even God is an admirer of Van Gogh.

Artists, and others, may accomplish God's business without even being aware that they are, and without a conscious motive of doing God's work. I know doctors who carry out their healing art as a gift to people, not really thinking that they may be doing God's work. I know carpenters and architects and a host of other people who bring beauty to the world and to our lives. Those who do it for the joy of accomplishing something worthwhile for others are also doing the work of God. I can't say if their work is a way of loving God, but I believe God loves them for reflecting His creative image within them.

Extravagant Love. How are we to understand the deed of Mary in pouring the expensive perfume on Jesus' feet when, as Judas observed, it could have been sold and given to the poor? If love is only about giving the cup of cold water, or visiting one in prison, how can we justify this extravagant act? Jesus praised Mary for her kindness to Him—beyond kindness. "She bought it so that she might keep it for the day of my burial. You always have the poor with you, but you do not always have me" (Jn. 12:7-8). Arguably, this was a symbolic cup of water in that it soothed a deeper need of our Lord. However, the pure devotion to Jesus, especially the extraordinary act of wiping His feet with her hair, certainly went beyond the mere act of feeding, clothing and visiting that we might be tempted to settle for. There was a dimension of just plain adoring Jesus.

Where the Journey Has Led. I began this study with the hopeful expectation that if I really thought about it long enough and deeply enough, I could arrive at a definitive answer to the question, "What does it mean to love God." No, I wasn't looking for a formula, just a deeper understanding of what loving God means. My thoughts took me first to the most ordinary of places imaginable—a potato patch in Illinois. Since the beginning of civilization mankind has been planting potatoes—or their regional equivalent—and harvesting the fruit of their labors. It was an ordinary experience, but one in which I experienced God.

My father, who fanned the flame of my interest in God, was no ordinary man. He labored—toiled really—in an iron foundry. He passed on to me a zest for life, and a love for God. I saw both, his toil to feed his children and his instilling love for life and God in his children, as expressions of his love for God.

My quest has led to encounters with people from all walks of life, some next door and others in distant places. I've been informed by history, notably that which is preserved in the Bible. I've been enlightened by friends and strangers. Much of my research has been a search within.

After confronting my own question of what it means to love God with all my heart, soul mind and strength, I come happily to the conclusion that while it's a good question, it can't be finally answered, at least not in this life. It's an ever-unfolding experience, initiated in a commitment to love God, then expanding in ways that only love can make possible and explain.

A Symphony in Motion. Loving God is a symphony in motion, perhaps being rewritten on the fly with even God enjoying the unexpected variations on the theme. Looking back over my life I can appreciate the beauty and wonder of loving God within my own limits, while celebrating the variations of loving God experienced and expressed by others. I imagine that I understand more of loving God than did my father, as he understood more than his father before him. It's my hope that those whose lives I touched along the way will rise to more lofty heights than I of understanding the depths of the mystery of loving God.

I fancy myself standing on my own mount, as did Moses, looking into the promised land of even greater vistas I shall never experience in this life. I take enormous satisfaction in knowing that others who come after me may be better prepared to enjoy its milk and honey than I, perhaps in part because of windows on God's love I have tried to open.

I do not envy those who follow—those who enter some future Promised Land—their enjoyment of the milk and honey. I have tasted the manna, the quail and even the ground-up gold of my own idolatry that were the rich experiences of my own wildernesses. I would not trade even the frustrating times of wandering for the estate bottled wine of the Promised Land. I have known the wealth of the wilderness, the riches of the redeemed, and the selflessness of celebrating and embracing even my own ordinariness. My ordinary life has been, and is, of celestial dimensions.

Here's the best part. So is yours—if you would recognize it and embrace it! Get on then, with the richest of human experiences—loving God with all your heart, soul, mind and strength.

Made in United States
Troutdale, OR
02/21/2025